Parenting on Point

Parenting
P*on*INT

Leading Your Family Along God's Path

JAMES C. WILLIAMS

ABINGDON PRESS / Nashville

PARENTING ON POINT
LEADING YOUR FAMILY ALONG GOD'S PATH

Copyright © 2002 by Abingdon Press

This book is printed on acid-free paper.

Library of Congress Cataloging-in-Publication Data

Williams, James C., 1947–
    Parenting on point: leading your family along God's path / James C.
Williams.
        p. cm.
Includes bibliographical references.
    ISBN 0-687-06354-X (pbk.: alk. paper)
    1. Parenting—Religious aspects—Christianity.   I. Title.
BV4529 .W57 2002
248.8'44—dc21

                                                                      2002006135

02 03 04 05 06 07 08 09 10 11—10 9 8 7 6 5 4 3 2 1

MANUFACTURED IN THE UNITED STATES OF AMERICA

To

the loving memory
of my son, Curt,
whose brief time on this earth is the light
that illuminates my path each and every day;

my wife, Carol,
who offers unconditional love to her family
each and every day—
you are the love of my life;

my daughter, Beth,
whose resiliency and strength are matched
only by her beauty and forgiving nature.
I am honored to be your father.

CONTENTS

ACKNOWLEDGMENTS

First and foremost, I want to express my deep love and appreciation to the following family members:

My mother, Barbara, and my late father, Frank, with love and appreciation for all the sacrifices you made for me.

My brother, Biff, and my sister, Ann, for always being there for me and my family.

My loving aunt, Elsie Fallansbee, who was my soul mate during my youth.

My mother-in-law, Meg, and my father-in-law, Ted, for loving and supporting our family for these many years.

Second, this book and its many stories would not have been possible without the help of many people, young and old, who were instrumental in getting me into my current vocation, giving me the encouragement to write this book, or helping to keep me on point when I was growing up. Special thanks to:

Sally Sharpe, my editor and friend, who was able to recommend improvements without changing the critical points contained in the book. Although she wants no credit, her fingerprints are on this book.

Rodger Dinwiddie, my boss and Executive Director of STARS-CYI. Rodger was willing to take a chance on hiring me even though my teaching experiences were limited. Since my initial hiring, he continues to foster my growth both professionally and personally.

The STARS Staff, who have taught me so many things about working with children and parents and have never asked for anything in return.

Dianne O'Neil, whose initial support as my administrative supervisor and constant support as my friend will always be appreciated. Dianne has always openly shared knowledge with me and has helped guide me to the star that God wants me to follow.

Walter Quinn, who, in his role as Director of Marketing for Cumberland Heights Rehabilitation Center, provided the initial funding for my parenting classes.

ACKNOWLEDGMENTS

Linda Locke, who is the Christian Education Director for Hermitage United Methodist Church and also my friend, has been my spiritual counselor and supporter over the last several years.

Ellie Fleming, who, as the leader of my youth group at Fox Chapel Presbyterian Church, helped me to feel God's love for the first time in my life.

Mr. and Mrs. Michael Berardino and Mr. and Mrs. Howard Aufderheide, the parents of my childhood best friends, who nurtured me and helped keep me on God's path.

Gerard Berardino, Howard Aufderheide, Dennis DeGroat, John Frey, Kelly and Dottie Byers, my dearest friends, for loving my faults as much as my good points and for always being a positive influence when the critical issues were at stake.

William Trapp, a friend of Curt's from Birmingham-Southern College who has taken it upon himself to be a member of my family. His love and laughter have helped me deal with my grief.

The fifth and sixth grade students of Middle Tennessee, both past and present, who make my job so rewarding and continue to give me love and support.

INTRODUCTION

DREAMS CAN COME TRUE

If you are reading this book, then a dream is coming true. What makes this dream so special is that it began at a time in my life when dreams had stopped coming true. This dream was different from other dreams. You see, it came from God. I firmly believe that God has a dream for each of us—a mission that only we can fulfill. For several years now, I have known that my mission is to help parents get back "on point"—on the path that God wants them to follow. This book is part of a larger effort to fulfill that mission. To understand the passion I have for this mission and the sincerity of my desire to help you become a better parent, you must know a little of my story. (I share only the main points here. For the full story, you may listen to track 3 on the enclosed compact disc.)

My Story

My life changed forever on November 11, 1995, when a drunk driver killed my nineteen-year-old son, Curt. That night I came to the full realization that God gives everyone the free will to choose. That night a man exercised his free will to choose, and he chose to drink and then drive his truck home while intoxicated. My world was shattered.

At the time, Curt was a sophomore at Birmingham-Southern College, where he was thriving. Meanwhile, back at home, I was having great difficulty enjoying the parenting experience with my sixteen-year-old daughter, Beth. I was frustrated because she did not "embrace my world" as I thought she should, and we fought all the time.

When the call came from the hospital in Birmingham on the night of Curt's accident, my wife, Carol, left immediately, and I waited to locate Beth, who was out on a date. A few hours later, Beth and I rode all the way to Birmingham without even talking. I sat in the front seat with my minister, and Beth sat in the backseat by herself.

Two days after Curt's funeral, God "opened my eyes." I realized for the first time how distant Beth and I had become. I realized that I needed to change as a parent or I was going to lose Beth, too.

Approximately six months after Curt's death, I was advised by my employer of twenty-three years that my business unit was being eliminated and I was losing my job. This action gave me the opportunity to reevaluate my life's work. The fact that this loss happened so soon after the loss of Curt helped to "open my ears" and enabled me to listen to God. I felt that God was leading me to make a difference in the lives of children and parents by combining my lifelong passion for outreach with my recent volunteer work for STARS (Students Taking a Right Stand), a nonprofit organization in the public school system whose mission is to help children make healthy lifestyle choices. So, with incredible support from my wife, Carol, the Nashville STARS Director, Rodger Dinwiddie, and the local drug education coordinator, Dianne O'Neil, I worked to develop a series of educational and motivational speeches and classroom presentations for children, followed by a series of parenting classes and workshops for adults. Ever since, I have been working full-time in the classroom, devoting my days to helping children and my evenings to helping parents.

For several years, parents taking my courses have told me that they want me to write a book. "We need a reference manual that we can look to when we are 'off course,' " they have said. "And we want you to write that manual for us." Well, finally, here it is. My dream is to serve God by introducing as many people as possible to the concept of "parenting on point."

What Is "Parenting on Point"?

The concept of "parenting on point" is the idea of being on course, heading in the right direction, going down the right path—the path that God wants us to follow. As parents, we're responsible for leading our children along this path. Proverbs 22:6 gives us this instruction: "Teach your children to choose the right path, and when they are older, they will remain upon it" (NLT). To do this, we must have a "map," a parenting plan, to guide us. This book will walk you through the process of creating your own personalized parenting plan—a plan that will help you and your family to stay on point. Having this plan won't keep you from making mistakes and getting off point at times. It will, however, keep your family anchored to the important values, principles, and beliefs that will redirect you and get you back on point.

I have learned that staying "on point" means being willing to make whatever adjustments are necessary in order to keep God in the center of our lives. I have also learned that it's much easier to stay on point when we truly learn to offer unconditional love and conditional trust to our children. Parents who offer unconditional love create an atmosphere of kindness in the home. Kindness is a contagious behavior, and it will significantly reduce the anger and conflict in your home. As that happens, you will find that parenting is more fun and rewarding than you ever imagined.

If I am successful in this book, you will feel as if we have become friends; and, like all of my "students," you will find yourself referring to me as Jim. I want you to feel like you are sitting in a comfortable couch and I am sitting across from you, sharing the wisdom and knowledge I have gained over the last eight and a half years. If you ever feel that you are being lectured, then you have my permission to give the book to a distant relative for Christmas! Seriously, my intent is not to lecture but simply to help you avoid some of the mistakes and missed opportunities I experienced while raising my own children. Occasionally, I will get up on my soapbox to drive home an important point or implore you to take a specific action— and you will be able to identify these times by the boldface print— but I promise that in very short order I will get down again! I also promise to provide plenty of practical tips and strategies, "Parent Points," that you can put into practice right away. Finally, you will find at least one "Scripture Link" in each chapter to help you anchor your newfound knowledge or insights to your faith.

I hope that you will laugh and cry as I share my life with you, that you will take away better skills to meet the many challenges you face as a parent, and that you will be motivated to use these skills. If you do, I promise that not only will you enjoy the parenting experience far more than I did, but also, through your new sense of love and commitment to your children, you will find it easier to stay on point. That will be proof positive that dreams can come true.

GETTING YOUR FAMILY ON POINT

Teach your children to choose the right path,
and when they are older, they will remain upon it.

—Proverbs 22:6 NLT

1

WHY THINGS ARE MORE DIFFICULT FOR PARENTS TODAY

Scripture Link

Live no longer as the ungodly do, for they are hopelessly confused. . . . they are far away from the life of God because they have shut their minds and hardened their hearts against him. They don't care anymore about right and wrong. . . . But that isn't what you were taught when you learned about Christ.
—*Ephesians 4:17-20 NLT*

[God's grace] teaches us to say "No" to ungodliness and worldly passions, and to live self-controlled, upright and godly lives in this present age.
—*Titus 2:12 NIV*

I have had the privilege of working with struggling students during their summer school sessions as well as young people who have come through the juvenile court system. I say "the privilege" because I have learned so much from them. I have found several common threads concerning their outlook on life and why they are either flunking out of school or teetering on the edge of being in the juvenile court system for a very long time. The most important common thread I have been able to identify is this: All of these young people lack a "North Star" to follow.

Every Family Needs a "North Star"

When my father was a navigator in World War II, he used the North Star to guide the plane. Similarly, families today need a "North Star" to guide them. When I am conducting parenting workshops, I always begin by drawing a star at the top of the board. This star represents a sense of direction for our children and our families; we can think of it as the moral center of the family—the foundational family value system, or the guiding moral values and principles. All members of the family must understand this star, and it must become part of their daily lives. In the next chapter I will say more about how to identify this star for your family, but for now, let's consider why the "North Star" is so important.

The idea that our families need something to guide them certainly isn't new. Only the metaphors behind the idea change. In his book *The 7 Habits of Highly Effective Families,* Stephen Covey says that our families need a compass. Without a compass—or a "North Star"—we allow our focus to shift from our children to other things; and when this happens, the family begins to break down. One of the first symptoms of this breakdown is a lack of meaningful communication between parents and children, which is the direct result of a lack of time spent together.

In 1997, Covey identified that the average parent spends only fifteen minutes a day having meaningful conversation with each child in the family. This startling statistic is even worse when you realize that only three of the fifteen minutes are spent saying something positive. This means that, at best, most parents have a potential of three minutes a day to focus on the family's compass—or to reinforce the family's "North Star" (moral center) for their children.

You might want to argue that things wouldn't be so bad if we parents spent all of the fifteen minutes reinforcing the "North Star," God's path for us. However, we must remember that if *any* of our comments in those fifteen minutes are negative, then there is a very high probability that our children will not listen to us. This is why it is so important that we not allow our conversations about right and wrong behavior to become opportunities for identifying all that is wrong with our children. Instead, we should use these conversations as opportunities to identify all that is right or good with our children and our families, and to encourage one another to follow the "North Star"—the family value system. Later in the book I will cover some of the many ways you can increase your time with your children. During much of this time together you will be helping your children "catch" your values. By catching the family values, the child will view them as his or her own values and, therefore, will have the desire to sustain them.

There's no question that less time spent together—and, consequently, a decrease in meaningful communication between parents and children—is a major reason why things are more difficult for parents today. We all know that it takes time to love, nurture, and guide our children. Having a "North Star" helps us to be intentional about giving our children and our families the time and attention they need and deserve. It keeps us focused on the course we must follow if we are to stay "on point" and lead our families along the right path, the path God wants us to travel.

Today's Greatest Parenting Challenge: The Artificial Star

Though time—or the lack of it—is a major parenting challenge today, there's an even greater challenge. The number one reason why it's more difficult for parents today to keep their families on point is that there is another "star" in our children's lives acting as a huge magnet, drawing them away from the North Star. Bill Oliver, creator of the video parenting course *Parent to Parent,* says that there have been three revolutions since the fifties that have put our families at risk. Essentially, they can be characterized by the familiar saying "sex, drugs, and rock 'n' roll." I like to think of these three revolutions, plus one more that I have identified, as the alluring "artificial star." Separately, they are like four great winds, each doing its part to blow our children a little farther off point.

1. Sex

The first great wind involves the "S" word—you know, that word we just dread talking about with our children. We can thank

OUR TRUE NORTH

GOD'S PATH

ARTIFICIAL STAR

THE FOUR GREAT WINDS

SEX

DRUGS

ROCK 'N' ROLL &
THE ENTERTAINMENT WORLD

VIOLENCE

Hugh Hefner and the entertainment world for bringing sex out of the closet. Yet even after sex started to become a more socially acceptable subject, many if not most parents failed to have one-on-one discussions with their children about sex. Instead, they continued to delegate the responsibility of sex education to other adults—primarily teachers. Unfortunately, by delegating the responsibility, parents missed the opportunity to talk about sex in the context of their value system.

My high school health class was taught by one of our basketball coaches. It was an all-boys class. For one semester we learned about good health, but what we really wanted to know was the female anatomy. We also wanted to know about our own bodies. Finally, the day came for us to discuss sex. As the class began, there were twenty-five boys who were ready to ask the second question. We just didn't want to ask the *first* question! There stood our coach in front of the class, wearing his basketball uniform, with sweat pouring off his temple. Finally, he got up the courage to make a statement. *Here it comes,* I thought. *Finally, my many questions will be answered!* Then the coach said that if any of us didn't know how to "do it," would we please raise our hand. Actually, that's the way I remember it; he probably said it a little more discreetly. But the impact was the same. No hands were raised by any of my classmates.

In the summer between my junior and senior years, I attended a one-week church camp at Grove City College. For many reasons, this camp changed my life. However, what I remember most fondly about this week was that we had a caring and sensitive conversation with one of the ministers about sex. He was able to bring God into the equation. He was able to listen to our questions—many of them being extremely comical—showing complete respect for us. He even talked about masturbation. I left that church camp knowing that at least there was one activity that wasn't going to send me to hell.

When my son, Curt, was ten years old, Carol decided that it was time for me to have the birds and bees conversation with him. She had talked to some of her friends who had said that their husbands and sons had already had "the talk." I went to the library and got a book that was supposed to be relevant for a ten-year-old boy. Looking back on this event, I now realize that the book was more appropriate for a five-year-old. Anyway, I took Curt through the book. I was very uncomfortable. Normally, Curt and I had meaningful conversations about sports only. Somehow I managed to get through it. I told him that sex is a wonderful experience—even better than hitting an ace in tennis. I told him why his mother and I did not have sex until we were married, and why we expected him to wait as well. I felt relieved when I left his room, and I felt proud, too. However, I now realize that I actually failed miserably. Why did I fail? After all, we had "the talk," right? I failed because the birds and the bees talk was not enough. The next talk we had about sex—this time in the context of his dating relationships—wasn't until his nineteenth birthday, eight months before he was killed.

As parents, we must discuss sex with our children *frequently* if we want them to catch our values, rather than society's values. As you well know, society and popular culture continually promote premarital sex—and many other destructive behaviors—as being acceptable and even desirable. According to the typical R-rated movie, sexual intercourse is okay in high school, and by college it's no big deal. This is why it is so important for us to talk regularly to our children about sex—and other sensitive subjects—in the context of our beliefs and value system. If we don't, we run the risk that our children will follow the alluring artificial star. If we do, the odds are high that our children will catch our values instead of society's values. Though the influence of the media is strong, it can be overcome. I say this with confidence because my twenty-three-year-old daughter has chosen to follow her mom's example, rather than society's example.

PARENT POINT
Talking with Your Child About Sex

1. Begin talking with your child about sex before he or she enters puberty. As puberty approaches, your child's questions and interest will increase. Take advantage of this opportunity.

2. When your child no longer uses the word "yuck" to describe the opposite sex and dating is on the horizon, increase the frequency of your talks. You will find that, eventually, the subject *will* become easier to discuss.

3. Generally speaking, moms are more comfortable talking with daughters and dads are more comfortable talking with sons. If you are a single parent with a child of the opposite sex, find an adult mentor of the same sex as your child—one who shares your values—and ask this person to talk with your child.

4. Always talk one-on-one, privately. Choose a time and place conducive to candid conversation. The last few minutes before your child leaves on a date is probably not the best choice! Many parents find it effective to have these talks during special, "just the two of us" times together.

5. In addition to educating your child about reproduction and sexual intercourse, talk about the emotional and spiritual aspects of physical intimacy. Discuss your beliefs and values regarding sex, including premarital sex and petting, and explain why you hold these beliefs. Though there are differing views on the subject, if your child asks, I recommend you tell your child the truth about your past choices, explaining why you made those choices and sharing any regrets you may have.

6. Be sure to talk about oral sex. Many young people today consider oral sex to be a safe alternative to sexual intercourse. Educators tell me that in many of our middle schools, eighth grade boys are promoting oral sex as a rite of passage for sixth grade girls. Though experts say that the number of girls who actually participate is low (5-10 percent), there is no way to calculate the negative impact of this degrading and demeaning practice on all young girls.

> 7. Let the experts help you. There are plenty of good educational and religious resources available on the subject. (Your local church and your child's school may be of some help.)

I now realize there was one important thing I did for Curt related to the topic of sex—though I was unaware of it at the time—and it was to teach him delayed gratification. I've since learned that the concept of delayed gratification has a direct correlation with sexual activity. The simple act of being able to wait for something is an asset that all children need to acquire before puberty. We teach our children to wait by not giving them everything they want and by helping them learn to earn, save, and spend money appropriately. When we teach our children to wait in this way before adolescence, they find it easier to say no to sex—and alcohol and drugs—as teens. And when we combine lessons in delayed gratification with frequent conversations about sex, we are well on our way to overcoming the peer pressure associated with the artificial star.

Please do not delegate the responsibility of teaching your children about sex to the schools or the church. It is your responsibility as a parent to have *ongoing* discussions about sex so that your family's North Star—your family's belief and value system—may light the right path for your children.

2. Drugs

A second great wind that can blow our children off course is drugs. I became a volunteer for STARS (Students Taking a Right Stand) strictly because of survey findings that indicated there were drugs in my children's high school. The truth is, there are drugs in or around virtually every school in the country—including our elementary schools. Yet so many parents don't want to believe it or choose to ignore it, naively believing that *their* children somehow will not be exposed to it. Thousands of experts agree with Bill Oliver when he says that, as parents, we will never be able to completely shield our children from drugs. I always tell parents that if they truly believe they can keep their children away from drugs (which is not the same as keeping them from *using* drugs), I have a piece of property in Florida I want to sell them!

So, what can you do as parents to help your children? Here are four proactive steps you should take:

1. Develop a clear understanding of the various drugs that your children will come in contact with and the dangers associated with them. (This can be accomplished by maintaining close contact with teachers and guidance counselors in your children's schools.)

2. Maintain a constant dialogue with your children about these drugs.

3. Help your children be able to say the magic word "no" over and over again by teaching them delayed gratification and building their self-esteem and confidence.

4. Reinforce the family's "North Star" which lights the way for your children and points them in a direction away from drugs; one of the most effective ways you can do this is by modeling appropriate behavior yourself.

An important part of steps 1 and 4 is recognizing that nicotine is also a drug. I have always known that smoking cigarettes is dangerous, and I stopped smoking in my early twenties after watching my grandmother die from emphysema; but I never considered nicotine to be a dangerous drug for kids until I became involved with STARS. I have come to realize that nicotine is a gateway drug for elementary aged children, and this realization has caused me to see cigarette smoking through a different set of eyes. A gateway drug is simply the first drug that children try; and for many, this gateway drug leads them to try other drugs, including inhalants, alcohol, and marijuana.

Many of the students I teach are torn apart inside because they have parents who use tobacco products. I find that children today are very knowledgeable about the dangers associated with smoking, as well as the dangers of secondhand smoke. One day I asked a classroom of fifth graders how many of them have been exposed to secondhand smoke at home, and the majority of them raised their hands. For our children to stay on point, we parents must follow the North Star ourselves. How can we tell our children that drugs like nicotine are harmful to them and that our family will always take the right stand against drugs, and then proceed to use tobacco products ourselves? This creates an internal struggle within our children.

Likewise, we need to consider the impact our use of alcohol has on our children. Because social drinking is an acceptable practice in our society, we need to be diligent in having a regular dialogue with our children about drinking. Because our children are learning in school that alcohol is a dangerous drug, we need to be proactive at home in addressing our children's questions and fears.

Parents always ask me, "When is the appropriate time to talk with my children about drugs?" Here are a few guidelines:

PARENT POINT
Talking with Your Child About Drugs

1. Do your homework before talking with your child about drugs. Be informed about the dangers associated with cigarettes, inhalants, alcohol, and narcotics. Excellent materials may be obtained from the National Clearing House for Alcohol and Drug Information (1-800-729-6686).

2. Whenever drugs appear in commercials, TV shows, or movies, use these opportunities to talk with your child about the dangers associated with these drugs.

3. Find out when the drug education program will be presented at your child's school, and talk to your child about the program that evening at home.

4. At least twice a year, discuss the subject of drugs at a family meeting. Rather than presenting a lecture, let this be a time of sharing information and answering your child's questions.

Please, please, please become educated about the drugs that are in your children's world; have regular discussions with your children about drugs; empower your children to say "no" by teaching them delayed gratification and building their confidence and self-esteem; and model appropriate behavior yourself.

3. Rock 'n' roll and the entertainment world

The third great wind that can blow our children off point is the entertainment world. The entertainment world is what makes the artificial star so attractive to our children. When we consider all it encompasses—music, books, television, video games, movies, the Internet—it's clear that society's wants and desires, rather than the family's needs, are the driving force behind the artificial star.

In 1997, Stephen Covey found that the average child in the United States was spending five to seven hours a day being entertained by this great wind *(The 7 Habits of Highly Effective Families)*. With the increased popularity and accessibility of the Internet, the number of hours may be even greater today. Though this "wind" involves a variety of entertainments, I want to focus on what I believe are the two most influential: music and television.

First, there was music. Long before there was television to contend with, music was influencing the youth of the world. We know from experience how much our own childhood and teen years were colored and shaped by the music we listened and danced to.

I didn't really start listening to music until I was in the fifth or sixth grade. Rock 'n' roll originals such as Elvis Presley, Chuck Berry, and Jerry Lee Lewis had just gotten their start. I listened to songs like "Green Door," "The Purple People Eater," and "Beep Beep," and groups like the Beach Boys, the Four Seasons, and, later, the Beatles. In college my favorite groups were Simon and Garfunkel, the Temptations, the Four Tops, and believe it or not, the Monkees. Although my parents didn't exactly share my musical tastes, they never asked me not to listen to the music I enjoyed hearing on the radio or on Dick Clark's *American Bandstand* television show. They never had any reason to! Though I'm sure there were songs being played that pointed to the artificial star rather than my family star, I honestly can't remember the words of those songs!

Today, children have so many more choices to make when it comes to the music they want to listen to. Although it's true that every generation has had its share of music that "pushes the envelope," so to speak, there's no question that the music popular among today's youth pushes the envelope more than ever before. The birth of the music video has only compounded the negative influence that certain music has on our children. Many of the music videos today have extremely graphic content and can create new social norms—in dress, behavior, and language. Now it's not only the lyrics of the songs that glamorize the artificial star but also the storylines of the music videos.

I can't say how much negative impact music will have on your children. I can say it is extremely important that you know what's going on in the world of music today; that you listen to the lyrics, watch the videos, and have an ongoing dialogue with your children about these things in the context of your family's values. As the saying goes, "It's always better to be safe than sorry."

Then, along came television. I was ten years old in 1957. We had only one television in the house. My mom controlled it until my dad came home from work. We had no remote control. Well, actually we did. "Jimmy, please get up and change the channel for me," my dad would command. In the morning, we would watch the *Captain Kangaroo* show before heading off to school. When we came home from school, we would watch the *Mickey Mouse Club*. (I was madly in love with Annette Funicello.) When Mickey was over, we were sent outside to play. You see, back then, the only organized sports for elementary school children came during the summertime; and my only other extracurricular activity, music lessons, was taught at school.

After dinner we were required to do our homework. If we needed our mom's help, we had to ask her early in the evening. My mom was a nursery school teacher, and she was tired by day's end. After helping us with our homework, she would go upstairs every evening to read a book while my dad would lie on the couch, listening to ball games or watching television with us kids. (To this day, my mom has little time for television.) I normally finished my homework by 8:00 P.M., and then I could watch TV shows with my parents until 9:00 P.M. Many of the classics were on at this time— shows like *Leave It to Beaver, Ozzie and Harriet, The Andy*

Griffith Show, and *Father Knows Best.* All of these shows had one thing in common: They all pointed me toward my family's North Star.

Times sure have changed. Today, instead of watching the *Mickey Mouse Club* when they come home from school, our children can watch soap operas or reruns of shows like *Roseanne.* Like the shows I watched as a kid, these shows all point our children toward a star—the *artificial* star. The artificial star tells us we should do what feels good, not what feels right. The artificial star says we should live for today and not wait for pleasures. These are the messages of the entertainment world.

Many people agree with Bill Oliver's claim that the entertainment revolution feeds the drug and sexual revolutions—and, I would add, the violence revolution, which I will address in the next section. The entertainment revolution keeps the others alive and growing. Just try to find prime time TV shows or PG movies today that don't have many sexual undertones or acts of violence. Or try to find a TV show or movie that doesn't show someone smoking a cigarette. Or count the beer commercials that air when a sporting event is being broadcast. It's around one out of three.

I often ask the fifth graders I teach to name a beer they know about because of seeing it on a TV commercial. All of their hands proudly go up in the air, and their faces light up like a Christmas tree. As they get older and the family's North Star is allowed to dim, many of these children will become active consumers of beer and other forms of alcohol. Sadly, the "pull" of the entertainment world is too great for many children to resist when they are not continually pointed toward the North Star, which helps to light the right path. Still, the entertainment world doesn't have to have the last word. In fact, Bill Oliver says that the entertainment revolution is the only societal revolution we parents can do something about. Forget about trying to eliminate sexual activities or drugs in our society today, he says; just help your kids to say no. However, there are things we can do to significantly reduce the negative impact of the entertainment world on our children. Here are a few suggestions.

PARENT POINT

Reducing the Negative Impact of the Entertainment World

1. Limit the amount of time your child spends watching TV/videos. Determine a reasonable daily limit and stick to it!

2. Don't use TV/videos as a babysitter; watch together.

3. Don't rely on the rating system used by the networks and film/music industries. Screen television shows, movies, music, and videos before allowing your children to see or listen to them. At the very least, evaluate the content by consulting reviews and Web sites that provide detailed information.

4. Always explain *why* certain content is inappropriate or unacceptable, discussing the material in the context of your family's values and beliefs.

5. Whenever you encounter inappropriate or unacceptable content while viewing a television show, video, or movie with your child, don't hesitate to change the channel or leave the theater! Then, use this opportunity to discuss and reinforce your family's values and beliefs. The same principle applies to listening to music at home or in the car.

In addition to changing our viewing and listening habits, we can take steps to bring about change in the entertainment world itself. There's so much that needs to be done. My generation got cigarette commercials off TV. Your generation can work to get smoking off sitcoms and movies—permanently. (Not long ago it seemed to be taboo, but now it's back.) Your generation can work to get beer commercials off TV. Your generation can work to reduce the amount of violence and sex on TV during prime time viewing hours. In short, your generation can help to "dim" the entertainment world so that the artificial star becomes a small, flickering star—just as it was when I was a boy. How? Write your congressional representative. Quit watching television shows and movies with unacceptable content. Boycott the products advertised to support these shows. As your children see you taking tangible steps to "put your money where your mouth is"—to support the beliefs, principles, and values important to your family—your family's North Star will grow and shine even brighter, lighting their way.

4. Violence

Bill Oliver suggests there are three revolutions—or winds, as I call them—that are negatively influencing the family. I believe there is a fourth: violence—both physical and verbal.

It surprises many parents to hear that verbal violence is a significant issue in their children's lives. I came to this shocking realization when I started asking students to raise their hands if they liked themselves and if they felt special. I was overwhelmed by the number of students who didn't raise their hands. After talking about this with teachers, principals, guidance counselors, and STARS personnel, I discovered that the words children hear are a major cause of low self-esteem.

Some of the most damaging words our children hear are the words that other children use to put them down. By the age of ten, children have developed the need to like the way they look. Sadly, many of the hurtful words their peers use to put them down deal with the way they look. By the age of ten, girls (and boys) begin to show signs of sexual growth. Sadly, many of the hurtful words boys use when they put girls down make them feel "dirty" inside. When I ask students what they think I remember more, the physical violence or the verbal violence I experienced as a fifth grader, 95 percent always say "verbal." And they're right. When I ask them to tell me which kind of violence bullies use most often to put them down, 90 percent say "verbal." Just like us, every child needs to have a friend; but, thanks to verbal violence, some feel as if they have no friends at all. Sadly, verbal violence is a problem not only in our schools but also in many of our homes as well, which we will discuss in detail in chapter 9.

Physical violence has also become a significant issue in our children's lives. Over the last several years we have witnessed an increase in horrific acts of physical violence committed by young people—many committed in our schools. (We will consider some of the common threads among youth who are at risk for violent behavior in chapter 10.) Most schools today have a zero tolerance on physical violence, and this is a helpful step in the right direction. If we are to dramatically reduce physical violence in the lives of our children, however, we must also reduce violence in the home—both verbal and physical—including our children's exposure to the violence promoted by the entertainment world. Although it is true that some youth can be exposed to high levels of "entertainment violence" and not become violent themselves, there's no question that repeated exposure to violence in TV shows, movies, and video games desensitizes youth—and adults—to the real violence in the world. And, as experts agree, exposure to violence through the entertainment world can cause a change in behavior—particularly in children, who don't always clearly distinguish between reality and fiction.

Essentially, the issue comes down to this: To what degree will our children be influenced by "entertainment violence"? The idea that even a small percentage of our young people have become numb or even immune to violence is very distressing to me. For them, violence doesn't appear real. It doesn't seem like the wrong choice. As parents, then, it is crucial that we create a nonviolent atmosphere in our homes by monitoring our children's exposure to the entertainment world, setting limits, and modeling appropriate behavior ourselves.

Please, please, please do not allow verbal or physical violence to be acceptable behavior in your house. And remember that violence can "sneak" into your home in the name of entertainment, which is why it is so important to monitor what your children watch. Let your family's North Star light a path leading away from all kinds of violence.

Which Star Will Your Family Follow?

As I've mentioned, when I was a boy, the artificial star was very small. It was more like a flickering, fading star. In contrast, my family's North Star was huge in size and followed me everywhere.

Today the artificial star is not only much larger than when I was a boy, it continues to grow in size every year. As parents, we have choices to make; we have priorities to set. These choices and priorities help to determine which star will be the biggest and brightest in our children's lives—which prompts me to get on my soapbox one more time.

We can continue allowing our children to spend hours a day with the artificial star, or we can reduce that time and replace it with time spent understanding the family star, the North Star. In the final analysis, this chapter comes down to one question: Which star does God want your family to follow?

QUESTIONS TO PONDER

1. Does your family have a "North Star" (a moral center, a family value system)? Does it represent *your family's needs* (emotional, spiritual, physical), rather than *society's wants*? Does every family member understand your North Star (as appropriate to his or her age)?

2. Do you model your family values every day? What does your behavior say about your values?

3. Do you have regular conversations with your children about your family values? Do you discuss difficult issues such as sex and drugs?

4. Do you smoke? Do you smoke around your children? Have you discussed smoking with your children?

5. Do you consume alcoholic beverages? Do you drink around your children? Have you discussed drinking with your children?

6. How much time does each of your children spend each day being entertained by television/videos, video games, music,

and/or the Internet? If you decide to reduce the amount of time your children spend being entertained, how will you fill the void?

7. Do know what TV programs/videos your children watch? How often do you watch—and discuss—these programs/videos together? Before you allow your children to see a TV show or movie, do you screen it first?

8. Do you tolerate any violence in your home—verbal or physical?

2

EVERY FAMILY NEEDS A
MISSION STATEMENT

Scripture Link

It takes wisdom to have a good family, and it takes understanding to make it strong. It takes knowledge to fill a home with rare and beautiful treasures.
                                                —Proverbs 24:3-4 NCV

Keep these words . . . in your heart. Recite them to your children and talk about them when you are at home and when you are away, when you lie down and when you rise. Bind them as a sign on your hand, fix them as an emblem on your forehead, and write them on the doorposts of your house and on your gates.
                                                —Deuteronomy 6:6-9

As I look back on my childhood, I can clearly see that my family had a North Star illuminating a clear path for me to follow, though I wasn't aware of it at the time. Perhaps because the artificial star was so small and so distant then, and because the community worked together to instill a common set of moral values, there wasn't a need to formalize our family's star in any way. We were not taught values; we "caught" them. My parents modeled their values, and the church and community reinforced them.

So, for the first eighteen years of my life, staying on the right path—or, as I sometimes say, staying "on the sidewalk"—was not a difficult task for me. I noticed that when I would stay on the "sidewalk," my parents and relatives would do special little things for me. My mom would make me homemade cookies, and my dad would take me to a few extra ball games. Though I always felt loved, I felt extra special when I was "on point" with the family star.

Of course, there were times when I, like all kids, would find myself off the sidewalk. Whenever I was "discovered" by my parents or by any adult in my community, I would get a quick "signal" and immediately return to the sidewalk. Many times the signal was nothing more than "the stare." After getting this stare, I would end up like the witch in *The Wizard of Oz* after Dorothy spilled water on her—you know, "I'm melting! I'm melting!" I firmly believe that my dad had a contract with all the adults who were part of my life. The contract said that they had his permission to put me back "on point." All of my friends' fathers had the same contract. As Forrest Gump says, "Stupid is as stupid does." It didn't take me long to understand that my life was much more fun when I stayed on the sidewalk—when I stayed on point.

Today, however, we live in a different world. Times have changed, the artificial star has grown exponentially, and we must be even more proactive in our parenting. Yes, values still are more "caught" than taught; but verbalizing and discussing these values is crucial if we are to stay focused and stand firm when that huge magnetic artificial star tries to pull our children—and us—off point. For this reason, I strongly urge you to create a formal family mission statement and hang it in your kitchen as a constant reminder of your family's values, beliefs, priorities, and expectations.

I first learned about the concept of family mission statements from Stephen Covey, author of *The 7 Habits of Highly Successful Families*. The more I thought about it, the more sense it made. I knew that in order to be successful, a company must have a mission statement. Why should the family be any different? During my twenty-three years in corporate America, I developed goals and objectives that supported the company mission statement. I also learned that when the company didn't follow the mission statement—when the company "strayed away" for a while—not only the profitability of the company was impacted, but also the morale of the employees. Likewise, when a family doesn't have a mission statement—or has one but doesn't follow it—the family strays away from the path that will keep them on point. Children need a clear sense of direction, and they need that direction to be articulated. A family mission statement does both.

This chapter will guide you through the process of writing your own family mission statement and help you to identify some valuable commitments necessary for putting your mission statement into action.

First, Avoid Common Mistakes

Stephen Covey suggests there are three "watch outs" when it comes to writing a family mission statement. First, don't write it without the children's involvement and then expect the children to observe it. In fact, this is the most common mistake parents make. It's very important to involve the children in the creation of your family's mission statement, as we'll soon see.

Second, "don't rush it." A good family mission statement requires at least two drafts and more than one family session. It's especially important to give family members adequate preparation time before coming together the first time to share ideas and begin drafting a statement. I would add that prayer should be an important part of the preparation process, especially for parents. Families who give their mission statement very little thought or prayer often realize later that they don't want to live out the key points of the statement.

Third, and finally, "don't ignore it." In other words, don't tell your children that the family is going to write a mission statement and then never do it. Your lack of commitment will speak volumes.

Now that we've covered the don'ts, let's move on to the do's.

Involve the Whole Family, and Try to Make It Fun

First and foremost, the family mission statement needs to be a family affair. One of the questions parents ask me most frequently is this: How old does a child need to be in order to participate in the process? I don't have a definitive answer, but I do have a few recommendations. First of all, parents whose children are not yet in elementary school should spend more time writing a mission statement for their marriage than they do writing a mission statement for the family.

Let me pause here to say that, actually, a marriage mission statement should be the first mission statement every couple writes. As Covey reminds us, we commit to a "mission statement" when we get married and repeat marriage vows. Today, many couples write their own vows. The mistake we all make is that we don't frame these vows and hang them on the kitchen wall! Seriously, we make a mistake by not looking to our wedding vows to identify a clear path or "star" to follow throughout marriage. We make a mistake by not allowing our vows to remind us that we need to have God in the center of our daily activities. Perhaps if we would take the wedding vows seriously as a society, we would reduce the rate of divorce. Ideally, then, a marriage mission statement should precede a family mission statement. Covey suggests that this mission statement should be updated each year.

Having said that, let me share my rule of thumb for writing a family mission statement if you have young children. If the children are capable of understanding the Golden Rule, then they're capable of understanding a simple family mission statement. The key is to keep it simple! Some families with young children simply adopt the Golden Rule, or some variation of it, as their family mission statement.

Once children are in elementary school, they are ready to be included in the development of a more involved family mission statement. It's important to include the children for several reasons. For starters, if you want your children to "catch" the core family values, which are reflected in the family mission statement, then they need to feel they are involved in the process of creating that statement. Like adults, children feel a sense of ownership in something if they participate in it. What's more, children can even make valuable contributions! Although their input will not be as sophisticated as yours, it will be just as important. In fact, children often mention one of the key elements I recommend all families consider including in their mission statements, which is the need to have more fun together. That's another great reason for involving children in the process. It can actually be a wonderful opportunity to have some fun together!

I recommend you combine the process of writing your first draft with a fun family weekend. If possible, find somewhere away from home where the usual family interruptions may be held to a minimum. I am partial to those reasonably priced suite hotels that have an indoor swimming pool, game machines, good food, and suites that have a separate living area with table and chairs. I was always at my best with my children when we were somewhere that helped me to forget my worries and enjoy their company. The idea, after all, is to enjoy the experience! If getting away for a couple of days is not a possibility, then I recommend you go to a local park for several hours on a consecutive Saturday and Sunday—or even for just one day. The most important thing is that you are away from all phones—home phones and cell phones. Take a picnic lunch, paper and pencils, and some outdoor "toys" for a little family fun. Do whatever you can to make the entire experience fun and memorable!

Identify the Key Elements

The first and most important step in writing a family mission statement is to identify the key elements of your family's North Star—those values, principles, expectations, and objectives that you believe are central to your family's ability to stay on point, on the path God wants you to follow. *The key elements of your North Star should be the key elements of your family mission statement.*

Before involving your children in this step, it is important for you, as parents, to prayerfully identify and discuss these key elements until you are in agreement. Trying to resolve disagreements in front of the children will only derail the process. You need to have a common voice of reason when working on the statement with your children. Here are a few helpful questions to consider:

- What are the key elements, or important beliefs, of our faith?
- What are the values and principles most important to our family?
- What kind of atmosphere do we want to have in our home?
- What kind of behavior do we want family members to demonstrate?
- What kind of changes do we need to make in our family to have more fun together?

Prior to your first family session, ask each child to make a list of responses to some or all of these questions. Give a few examples.

Explain that the purpose of the mission statement is to identify or communicate your family's core beliefs and values—in other words, those things that your family stands for and believes in. To ensure that all family members participate, you may need to help younger children with their lists. Plan your day or weekend family getaway, and take your lists with you. Then, in your first working session, use the lists as a "jumping off place" for your discussion. You might find it helpful to give an example from your own list.

I always begin the discussion in my parenting classes with this example: A family should love one another. Then I add this important adverb: unconditionally. You may find this is a good place to start your family discussion as well. Talk about what it means to love one another unconditionally. Unconditional love requires us to love one another even when we disappoint each other. Unconditional love helps us to separate the behavior from the person. Unconditional love requires us to forgive one another and apologize when we are wrong. Throughout life, others will do things that disappoint us. No matter how bad someone's behavior may be, we should direct our anger at the behavior, not at the person. This might lead to a discussion of the other kinds of behavior you expect from one another.

Throughout this first session, your role as parents is to facilitate the discussion of the key elements, or values, to be included in your family mission statement and how your family should uphold or "live out" these values. Though you should encourage your children's input and incorporate their ideas as appropriate, you should not negotiate the key elements you identified and agreed upon in advance.

Before you begin this first step, let me suggest some key elements every family should consider.

1. Get back to the basics.

When our family lived in Pittsburgh, Chuck Noll was the head coach of the Pittsburgh Steelers. Under his leadership, the team won four super bowls. Occasionally, however, they would lose to a team they should have defeated. Following the game Coach Noll would always say that it was time to get back to the basics and practice blocking and tackling. Blocking and tackling are "the basics" for a football team.

What are "the basics" for families? When I think of the basics, I think of the things my own parents expected of my siblings and me. These expectations were the basics or the key elements of my childhood North Star, which helped to keep me on the sidewalk. As I've mentioned, my family didn't have a mission statement; but if we had, these four basic values would have been reflected in it. They are timeless basics that still have great value for families today.

First, my parents expected us to live by the Ten Commandments. Although they never sat down and reviewed the commandments with us, we learned them at church and we saw them lived out in our parents' lives—and we knew they were "the law of the land." Unfortunately, society tends to undervalue the Ten Commandments today. Someone once said that because so many adults commit adultery these days, children no longer consider the commandment "Thou shalt not commit adultery" to be the "law of the land." Unfortunately, the same could be said for each of the other commandments. Judging from the sitcoms on TV today, you might think there were no commandments at all. In fact, I recommend hanging a copy of the Ten Commandments on the kitchen wall right next to the family mission statement!

Second, my parents taught us to live by the Golden Rule—to treat others the way we wanted to be treated. There were many times that I didn't want to follow the Golden Rule. When people were mean to me, I found myself wanting to strike back. And there were times when I saw someone else being bullied but didn't stand with the victim. However, because I knew that this principle came from God, and because I believed in the concept of heaven and hell, I would always feel guilty and do something to make things right. Besides, as I've mentioned, I knew that the adults in my life had my parents' permission to give me a quick consequence if they ever saw me breaking the Golden Rule!

Most parents today have at least heard of the Golden Rule; unfortunately, many only pay lip service to the principle and don't encourage their children to stick out from the crowd and follow it. Those who are in the popular cliques generally don't follow the Golden Rule, and those who know how to get ahead—otherwise known as bullies—don't follow it, either. So while we're framing the Ten Commandments, we should frame the Golden Rule—and, yes, hang it on the kitchen wall!

Third, my parents expected us to always give our best effort. Thank goodness that effort was more important to them than grades! My older brother got straight A's, as did my younger sister. With great pride, I introduced my parents to C's. Then, in college, I got my first D (Political Science), but I was able to convince my parents that I had given the class my best effort. Today, a child's best effort should still be good enough. In most cases, if students give subjects their best efforts, they are able to earn the grades necessary for acceptance into college. This leads me to another expectation of my parents, which was closely related.

Fourth, my parents expected me to go to college—"case closed," as they would say. Because my father's father was an alcoholic, my dad took on the responsibility of helping his mom from an early age. As a result, he never graduated from high school. After serving in World War II, he worked with his dad at the car dealership. My mom graduated from one of those "snobby" schools: the Connecticut College for Women. There could not have been a greater contrast between the two. However, I think the desire for me to go to college was even more important to my dad. He truly wanted more for his children. My mom always went out of her way to tell us how smart our dad was. For our family, college was not a sign of intelligence; it was a mountain that we needed to climb. You might say that it was the best way of ensuring that we would always do our best.

Through the years, these were the basic values my parents tried to instill in me, and, eventually, they became my own. I "caught" them, and I never threw them back. Fortunately, I didn't have a huge artificial star pulling me off the sidewalk. Unfortunately, our children do. That's why it's so important to get back to the basics—and equally important to include these basics in your family mission statement. Writing a family mission statement that communicates your family's basic beliefs and values is one of the best ways to help your North Star outshine the artificial star.

2. Put faith and family first.

In her book *Winning the Parenting Game: Putting Family First,* Deloris Jordan, mother of basketball's Michael Jordan, explores the many universal goals that parents should set for their children—goals such as self-discipline, responsibility, perseverance, the desire to achieve, and moral values. I believe it's impossible to help our children realize these goals, however, unless we do as the title of her book suggests and put family first. I also would add faith to the equation. Putting faith and family first is a key element that should be part of every family's North Star and mission statement.

There's a story I like to share with parents because it's a classic example of not putting faith and family first. When Curt was six and Beth was three, my back went south on me. I had a lot of pain whenever I would sit. Right before accepting a transfer to Spartanburg, South Carolina, I had an operation. It failed. My new job in Spartanburg was ten times more stressful than my job in Pittsburgh had been. I was working ten to twelve hours a day—plus Saturdays. When I wasn't at work, I was at the YMCA, trying to exercise and strengthen my back. On top of my work problems and my back pain, I had to deal with the stress of having an unhappy family. Spartanburg was not a friendly town to the Williams family; we never felt accepted. We had five miserable years there.

Things in Pittsburgh had been so different. We had a mortgage that allowed Carol to stay at home with the kids. Curt and Beth loved their schools and had a lot of friends. Their best friends lived right next door. We had neighbors on the other side of our house who didn't have any children, and they loved ours as if they were theirs. My parents lived thirty minutes away, and we had dinner with them every Sunday. I also had loving aunts and uncles who lived close by. Carol's family lived only three hours from us. We were very active in a small church. I was chairperson of the outreach committee, and we were doing wonderful things. The congregation was very loving and cared deeply for the children in the church. When I started having back problems, there were many people who helped me to deal with it. Our family was surrounded by loving and caring people, and we felt totally accepted by our community.

Can you imagine why we would give all that away? Later, as I became more knowledgeable about the critical elements of a successful family, I looked back on our decision to leave Pittsburgh with much guilt and shame. The answer can be boiled down to one word: promotion. I was offered a promotion to move to Spartanburg and start two new companies from the ground floor. I was the first controller ever chosen who didn't have an accounting degree. My boss was very proud of my appointment, and so was I. I guess there is another word that explains why we moved: ego.

In one of my parenting classes, a man asked why I didn't quit the company and return my family to Pittsburgh. The truth is, we never discussed that option as a family. How could we admit that we had made a big mistake? How could we face the scary idea of starting all over again with a new company? Actually, I probably could have gotten my old job back. I guess I don't really have an answer for his question. What I realize now is that if we had written a family mission statement after the birth of our two children, and if that mission statement had included a sentence about always putting faith and family first, then I am absolutely sure we never would have left Pittsburgh.

Too often we make decisions that benefit one member of the family at the expense of the others. Careers seem to be the culprit most of the time. Moving from Pittsburgh was a great career move for me, but the other members of my family suffered. I didn't realize at the time how important it was for the children to feel accepted in their neighborhood and their schools. I didn't realize that some children adapt well to moves while others do not. If possible, it's better to move before your children enter their crucial years of development, which most experts say are between the ages of ten and fourteen. If a younger child has a hard time adapting after a move, then another move is probably not a good idea. If your job requires you to accept transfers, then ask yourself this question before making a move: "Will this transfer prevent us from keeping our faith and family first?" If so, I recommend you consider other employment opportunities. A job or career change made on behalf of the family's best interests can be cathartic not only for the wage earner but also for the entire family. Remember, putting faith and family first means making decisions that are good for the entire family.

Putting faith and family first also means finding a church that meets the spiritual needs of every family member. It means not only going to church together but also discussing and living out the beliefs of your faith—beliefs such as the Ten Commandments and the Golden Rule. It means giving generously to the church (if possible, practicing tithing) and making church activities a high priority despite competing demands. After all, what better way is there to put faith and family first than to be involved in the life of the church *together?*

Please, please, please don't make the mistake of letting anything become more important than your faith and your family.

3. Develop and support family members' gifts and talents.

Another key element many families include in their mission statement is developing and supporting family members' gifts and talents. Each of us has one or more God-given gifts or talents. When we do these things, we feel God's love for us. Developing and supporting one another's gifts and talents, then, is a way to increase our opportunities for feeling God's love for us.

Let me pause to acknowledge, however, that gifts and talents are certainly not the only activities that allow us to feel God's love for us. Sometimes we feel God's love when we're doing things we're not very good at! For example, I love to sing, but I sound like a frog croaking on a lily pad. Still, when I sing hymns in church, I feel God's love. Likewise, many children enjoy singing but aren't great singers. This is why we need youth choirs that allow all children to sing. Other children like to play sports but can't make the school team. This is why our churches need good athletic programs that allow all youth who come to the practices to play an equal amount of time in the games. I believe that whenever children feel good about themselves, they are more capable of feeling God's love for them. So, our objective should always be to help our children to feel good about doing their best, rather than make them feel they must be the best.

Helping our children identify and develop their gifts and talents is an excellent way to help them feel good about themselves. Sometimes our children's gifts and talents are obvious, but sometimes they are hidden away, waiting for the opportunity to be exposed. This is why it is important for us to encourage our children to try many things—music, painting, sports, dancing, and so forth. Through the years, I've observed that we tend to look for the gifts or talents in our children that we can relate to, rather than for those that may be "below the surface." We'll discuss this in more detail in chapter 10.

In addition to helping our children identify and develop their gifts and talents, we should show our support through our interest and our presence. I encourage you to attend as many of your children's games, recitals, and programs as you possibly can, being careful not to promise you'll be there unless you can keep that promise. (As we'll discuss in chapter 10, younger children consider a promise to be a covenant, a sacred trust; and we lose their trust when we break a promise.) It is not necessary, however, to attend all the practices or rehearsals. Though it's a good idea to attend a couple of practices in the beginning to make sure that the teacher's/coach's methods are in sync with your values, it's not advisable to go to every practice because that usually means someone in the family has to suffer. Sometimes it's you when your schedule is stretched even tighter, and sometimes it's a sibling who has to tag along. Whenever possible, however, do encourage siblings to attend games and recitals to show their support as well. Carol was the one in our family who ensured that supporting the children's gifts and talents was a "family thing." Curt had to go to all of Beth's dance recitals, and Beth had to go to all of Curt's tennis tournaments.

In addition to developing and supporting our children's gifts and talents, we need to be sensitive to our own gifts and talents. Be sure that your family mission statement emphasizes supporting all family members' gifts and talents. It also should state that each family member is responsible for using his or her gifts and talents. When parents tell me they don't have time to develop their gifts or talents, I say, "Then you're not putting your family at the top of your priority list!" You see, to be the best parent you can be, you need time for yourself. To be the best parent you can be, you need to do things that make you feel close to God.

Developing and supporting one another's gifts and talents, then, is a good way to keep the entire family on point.

4. Have more fun together!

When I am brainstorming with parents, I often ask, "What will be the first thing your children will want to include in the family mission statement?" Most of the time, parents agree that their children will say they want the family to do more fun things together. The idea of having more fun may seem a bit simplistic or even juvenile for a family mission statement, but the truth is that too many families simply don't enjoy one another. I certainly wish I had been able to enjoy parenting more. I never was able to leave my work at the office. It's not that I did a lot of work at home; it's that I brought the stress home. I didn't realize that having a little more fun at home would work wonders—not only for me, but also for my family.

Until "the light came on," I struggled with finding family activities that everyone enjoyed. When we lived in South Carolina and none of us had any close friends, we needed to concentrate on keeping the family unit together. I remembered how much fun I had had as a boy, boating on Lake Erie with my family. My grandfather had bought a boat when I was very young, and I had used that boat even into my young adult years. In Spartanburg, we didn't have enough money to buy a boat, so we shared a boat with another family. They had two daughters, so Curt wasn't very excited about the idea at first. But in time, he discovered that out on the lake, it wasn't so bad to be with the girls! Eventually that family moved away, but we decided to keep the boat. The best part about the boat was that it didn't have a radio. Once we were on the lake, we talked to one another, played with one another, and enjoyed one another's company. Some of our favorite family stories we still share today are about that boat.

Because Curt was the older child and was very athletic, he learned to slalom first. One summer Curt was away, and Carol and I were on the lake with Beth. "Dad, I want to learn how to slalom!" Beth exclaimed. Oh, no, I thought, she's too young, and it will be a very aggravating day for me. First, we tried it her way— trying to get out of the water on one ski, just like Curt. Then we tried it my way—kicking off one ski after getting up on two. By then it was late in the afternoon, and Beth and Carol convinced me to let her try it again her way. Three tries later she got up on one

47

ski and was incredibly good at it. We all had a big hug when she got back into the boat. The next weekend we had Curt with us. We didn't tell him about Beth's success. In front of Curt, Beth asked me if she could try to slalom. "Oh, no, Beth!" Curt exclaimed. "You are not old enough to try." I told Beth that she could try, but just for a short time. While Beth was in the water, Curt was telling me all the reasons why Beth would not get up. Beth gave me the okay sign, and I hit the throttle. Up she popped. I will always remember the look on Curt's face—and the look on Beth's face when she got back into the boat!

One time I forgot to put the plug in before backing the boat into the water. Curt was in the boat, and I was driving the car. We had an automatic bilge pump in the boat. All of a sudden I heard Curt yell, "Dad, we seem to have a small leak!" I looked in my rearview mirror and saw the bilge pump throwing out water reminiscent of Niagara Falls! Perhaps that's why my kids began calling me Chevy—after Chevy Chase in the movie *Vacation*—whenever they would retell stories about me putting the boat in the water each spring. Naturally, I smiled when a father recently told me that his family had bought a used boat, and it was the best decision they had ever made!

Please, please, please do something fun together on an ongoing basis that will bring the family together, such as hiking, camping, biking, or whatever—just do *something*. You will never be able to measure the dividends from this investment.

PARENT POINT
Writing a Family Mission Statement

1. Introduce the key questions.

2. Have a brainstorming session.

3. Identify common threads.

4. Put the common threads into salient points (first draft).

---

5. Review with family.

6. Make revisions and finalize.

7. Print it, frame it, hang it.

8. Identify core commitments, which are your yearly goals and objectives.

9. Print them and post them.

Put It in Writing

Once you have identified the key elements to be included in your family mission statement—those things that are central to your family's ability to stay on point—then you are ready to write your first draft. I recommend that you begin your statement with a very simple phrase, such as, "It is the mission of the Williams family to . . ." Then, communicate your key values in a series of phrases, each separated by a bullet. For example:

It is the mission of the Williams family to:
• respect each other at all times
• follow the Ten Commandments
• love each other unconditionally
• follow the Golden Rule
• go to college
• respect our elders
• (and any others)

Please remember, however, that this is only one approach; there's no right or wrong format to use. Your mission statement should reflect your family's own style and personality.

After you've written the first draft, it's time to "let it simmer" a while. I suggest one to two weeks. Post the draft in place where everyone can see it, such as on the refrigerator or a family message board. Then, once everyone has had time to give it some thought, hold another family session and make any final revisions.

Now you're ready for the final step.

Identify Core Commitments

Once you've made your final revisions, it's time to identify the specific commitments you must make in order to support your mission statement. You might say that these core commitments are the "action plan" necessary for implementing or living out the key elements of your mission statement. As I learned in the business world, a mission statement alone isn't enough. Just as every business unit must develop an annual business plan to support its mission statement, so also every family must develop an annual action plan to support their mission statement. Using this concept, I have developed a list of core commitments that I think every family must adopt in order to support the typical family mission statement. Of course, your family may choose to add other commitments to the list that will help you to support the unique aspects of your mission statement. If your family will review and renew your mission statement and the corresponding core commitments each year, I am confident that you will be successful in putting your family mission statement into action.

1. Make a commitment to a moral framework.

As I've already mentioned, the Ten Commandments and the Golden Rule are an excellent foundation for a moral framework. Some families choose to include the new commandment of Jesus (Matthew 22:37-40) and other Bible verses, as well.

2. Make a commitment to your church.

If worshiping as a family is a key element of your mission statement, then it's important for your family to make a serious commitment to your church. In addition to making a commitment to attend weekly worship as a family, I recommend that each family member make a commitment to participate regularly in Sunday school and at least one other church activity.

3. Make a commitment to family time.

If we are going to make family our highest priority (along with faith), then we must make a commitment to family time. That's why it is so important to be intentional and deliberate about making a commitment to family time. Begin by determining what the minimum amount of family time should be each week—as well as the minimum amount of "couple time," without kids. Then, hold one another accountable.

4. Make a commitment to a healthy lifestyle.

We know that our health, as well as the health of each family member, affects the way we live and interact with one another on a day-to-day basis. Consider the specific requirements you want your family members to satisfy related to food, exercise, sleep, physical checkups, and so forth.

5. Make a commitment to safety.

Safety, like health, is so important to family life. This commitment should include testing fire extinguishers and smoke alarms, having an escape plan, locking up inhalants, having annual car checkups or inspections, and setting family rules about alcohol and other drugs.

6. Make a commitment to education.

Though it may seem obvious, it's important to make specific family commitments regarding education for both children and parents. Education helps us to keep our minds sharp and to set and achieve important goals. As parents, we need to model the importance of education for our children.

7. Make a commitment to a family banking system.

Making a commitment to a family banking system helps you to reduce conflict in the home and keep your focus on your family's values and priorities. One of the most important aspects of a family banking system is a family budget. We will discuss this and other aspects of the family banking system at length in chapter 7.

It's Up to You

I hope that the key elements and core commitments suggested in this chapter will be helpful to you as you write your own family mission statement and core commitments. Remember that no two families are exactly alike, and no two family mission statements or lists of core commitments will be identical, either. Take what you will from this chapter and adapt it for your family, adding those ideas, goals, or objectives that are unique to your family. If the environment is important to your family, for example, you might reflect this in your family mission statement and live out your commitment through family activities such as recycling and adopting a street in your community to keep free of litter.

I consider creating a family mission statement and the corresponding commitments to be the most important aspect of getting your family on point. Writing a mission statement is the best way to help all family members identify and understand your family's "North Star" and, consequently, be able to stay "on point." It's up to you.

QUESTIONS TO PONDER

1. What are the key elements of your family's North Star?

2. What commitments are you willing to make so that you will "walk the walk" and "talk the talk" when it comes to your family's North Star and mission statement?

3. Identify the adults who have influence with your children. Do they have the same values as your family?

4. What changes do you have to make as a family in order to put your faith and family first?

3

WHICH CHILD IS YOURS?

Scripture Link

Even children make themselves known by their acts.
—Proverbs 20:11a
Whoever welcomes this child in my name welcomes
me. *—Luke 9:48a*

A fundamental aspect of getting and keeping your family on point is recognizing and understanding the unique differences in the children God has given you. A course in personality differences and human behavior should be a requirement for all parents! I regret deeply that I did not know more about what drives children's behavior when my own children were young. If I had, the parenting experience would have been a lot less stressful and much more fun and rewarding. My intent in this chapter is to help you benefit from some of the key insights I have since gained by studying the work of experts on the subject (see the bibliography) and by reviewing my own parenting experiences with two very different children.

In all the parenting courses I teach, the favorite session continues to be on understanding children's behavior. Perhaps this is because, at one time or another, all parents wonder why their children behave the way they do! As surprising and confusing and frustrating and entertaining as children's behavior may sometimes be, you don't need a degree in child psychology to understand children better. Though all children demonstrate different behaviors at different times (just observe any child for twenty-four hours!), and some children demonstrate significant behavioral changes as they get older, most children fall into one of three categories or "types" (with the exception of children who have learning or behavioral problems such as Attention Deficit Disorder and Attention Deficit Hyperactive Disorder). My own children serve as perfect examples of the first two types. Type three is not evident at birth but develops over time. As I paint a picture of these three types of children, I hope you will be able to identify your own children somewhere in the mix.

The Compliant Child

My son, Curt, was what experts call the easy or compliant child. There are no books written about the Curts of the world. Curt immediately liked our family's value system. He "shook hands with it"; he embraced it; he "looked it in the eyes" and said that they were going to get along just fine. You might say he was weird. We told him to do something, and, most of the time, he did it. We could give him "the stare"—the same one my parents gave me—and he would respond.

I gave God no credit for the creation of Curt. I thought I had done it all by myself, with a little help from Carol. Oh, I was so proud of myself! When Curt was a young boy, I would take him to the mall to "show him off." He wouldn't misbehave like many of the other children at the mall. People would notice his good behavior and jokingly offer to trade their child for Curt. *No way, Jose,* I would think, congratulating myself that he was a great child because I was a great parent. Of course, I've since learned that compliant kids basically raise themselves—unless we get in the way, that is. In other words, if we point them in the direction of the family's North Star and provide the proper guidance, they willingly stay on point.

In their book *Parenting with Love and Logic,* Foster Cline and Jim Fay say that, in theory, the proper way to guide or raise a child can be compared to an upside down triangle. The point of the triangle, which is at the bottom, represents when the child is born; and the base of the triangle, which is at the top, represents the child's eighteenth birthday. The space within the triangle represents responsibilities, privileges, and freedoms. When the child is young, there are many more limits and boundaries than there are responsibilities, privileges, and freedoms. As the child gets older, we naturally give him or her more "space"—increasing the responsibilities, privileges, and freedoms while decreasing the limits and boundaries. When we follow this model with compliant children, they quickly learn that their good behavior brings positive results, including more responsibilities and freedoms. This, in turn, empowers them to make even more good choices and decisions. Later I will discuss how some parents make the mistake of imposing unreasonable restrictions on their compliant child during the teen years, causing the child to walk away from the North Star. So, even with compliant children, it is important to know how to apply reasonable and effective limits and consequences, which we will cover in detail in chapters 5 and 6.

Two years and four months later, Carol and I made a "big mistake." (Whenever I say this, I always have a big smile on my face!) You know what that mistake was, don't you? That's right: We decided to have another one.

The Strong-Willed Child

Unlike Curt, our daughter, Beth, didn't "shake hands" with our value system. She didn't embrace it. Instead, she "looked it in the eyes" and said that they weren't going to get along at all. The first words out of her mouth were "no" and "why." She is what James Dobson calls a strong-willed child. Truth is, the only reason many parents attend my parenting classes is that they have one or more strong-willed children and are desperate for help!

When I think back, I realize that I was angry with Beth even before she was born. You see, she wouldn't come out! With Curt, the delivery had been a breeze. Carol had had an epidural, and he basically had slid out. We actually had had fun during labor and delivery. I even took pictures. Carol tells people that I treated the occasion as if we were at Myrtle Beach. It was a different story with Beth, however. Carol had blood pressure problems from the very start. They had to stop the epidural, and I became its replacement. I stood behind Carol's head; and as she had a contraction, she would grab my neck and pull my head toward her abdomen. She said some unkind words about my heritage. I finally got tired of this procedure, ran to the side of the bed, and yelled to the womb, "Get out! Get out now!" I can imagine Beth in the womb with her arms crossed, thinking that she would come out when she was good and ready.

Even from infancy, it was clear that Beth was a strong-willed child. She had an incredibly high level of energy and, unfortunately, gave up naps at a very young age. (We all know that naps are as beneficial for us as they are for the child!) Curt, on the other hand, was still taking a nap at fours year old. As she grew, I would tell Beth not to cross a line, and she would cross it. Sometimes she would cross it with a big smile on her face. I would then increase the volume of my voice, but she would cross the line again—this time with an even bigger smile on her face! Whenever I would ask her to do something, she would always ask, "Why, Daddy?" I would find myself losing my temper and screaming, "Because I told you to do it; that's why!" I so much wanted to have "Daddy's little girl"—you know, a sweet little "doll" who would sit on my lap and tell me how much she loved me. But that was not the kind of child God gave me.

When Beth was three, we lived at the bottom of a steep hill. She had one of those three-wheel minitricycles made of plastic. It was low to the ground, and she could peddle it very fast. I told her that she was not allowed to ride it down the steep hill. Instead, she had to stay on our flat driveway. One evening I came home from work and heard her yell, "Hi, Daddy! Hi, Daddy!" I looked out the car window and saw Beth barreling down the hill on her tricycle. She was going as fast as the car! I got angry and stepped on the accelerator. She merely lifted her feet off the pedals so that she could go faster. Then I saw danger ahead. At the bottom of the hill was a large post—with a mailbox attached to it! I started to scream, "Watch out! Watch out for the mailbox, Beth!" Just before she was about to hit the post, she turned the handlebars ever so slightly and into the driveway she went. As an extra special treat for me, she did a series of donuts. As I got out of the car, she gave me a big smile. If only I had had that episode on film when she came to me to ask if she could get her driver's permit! If you have a strong-willed child, take lots of home movies. They will come in handy later!

I often joke that God must have a lousy sense of humor because, as I have learned through my studies, he gives us five

"Beths" for every "Curt" that is born. I also have learned that there is no relevancy to the theory that the first-born will be a compliant child and the second-born will be a strong-willed child. It's like a crapshoot. The genes are put into a shaker, and out comes a child. I have drawn this conclusion by surveying the parents in every class I have taught over the last six years. Though I do not believe that birth order determines children's personalities, I do believe that it has a lot to do with our approach to parenting. Obviously, we are more confident with the second child—and even more so with subsequent children. This is why it is so important for us to pay close attention to each child's own personality and adapt our parenting approach in order to help that particular child stay on point.

Unfortunately, I didn't understand why Beth was different from Curt. I wish that I had. I wish that I could go back and have another chance at raising Beth. If I had had the awareness that I have now, I could have enjoyed the process so much more; and Beth would have been a happier child as well. I made many mistakes with Beth, but perhaps the worst mistake of all was trying to raise her the same way I was raising Curt. My approach was to do things my way—or else. I failed to realize that every child is a unique child with unique, God-given gifts and, therefore, the way we interact with each child must be unique. (We will discuss how we can cultivate our children's gifts in chapter 10.)

Instead of embracing and celebrating Beth's differences, I challenged them. I always compared her to Curt. I wanted her to be an athlete, just like Curt. The problem was that she didn't particularly like sports. And because sports were about the only subject I felt competent to discuss with my children, Beth and I didn't talk very much. As she reached early adolescence and started pulling back from me, I gladly let her go. One day I found myself saying under my breath, "I don't like you." In other words: "I love you, but I don't like you. I don't like the clothes you wear; I don't like your friends, particularly your boyfriends; I don't like your attitude; and I don't like the fact that you argue with me over almost every rule and boundary that's in your life." When I share this in parenting classes, I see many parents hang their heads in shame because they have had the same feelings. "Keep your heads up!" I exclaim.

"You still have a chance to make your relationships with your children more rewarding and easier to maintain. You don't have to make the same mistakes that I did."

I was an inflexible parent who had no desire to learn about strong-willed children. I had no desire to see the world through Beth's eyes. I didn't negotiate. I didn't compromise on the little things, and I paid dearly for it. It all came to a head one terrible night, November 11, 1995. Beth was going on a date that night. As usual, we argued about my need to know where she would be. And, as usual, she said she just didn't know. When I became a bit ill tempered with her, she shouted her typical response: "Don't you trust me, Dad?" Eventually, I threw in the towel and told her that I didn't want to fight about it anymore. That night I didn't require her to tell me where she was going; she just had to be home by the midnight curfew.

When Carol got the call from the hospital in Birmingham, Alabama, telling her that Curt had been in a very serious car accident, I couldn't go with her. I needed to stay at home because I didn't know Beth's whereabouts. A couple of hours and many phone calls later, Beth arrived on the front porch with our minister. He told me that he was going to drive us to Birmingham. On that three-hour trip, I never said one word to Beth. I didn't even sit with her. I put her in the backseat, and I sat up front with our minister. Although Beth didn't know at the time that Curt was near death, I will always carry to my grave the guilt of not being there for her in such a great time of need.

After Curt's death, I was able to see the world through Beth's eyes for the first time. I realized that she was hurting as much as I was. It pained me to see that, within six months, her boyfriend dumped her because she wasn't very much fun to be around anymore. I began to change as a dad, and, luckily for me, she responded. I almost created a rebel (which we will discuss in the next section); but because Beth was able to forgive me and allow me to change, she never rejected our core family values. Today she is an incredibly resilient young woman who has a bright "star" lighting her path and a never-ending supply of unconditional love from her mother and dad. One of my greatest regrets, however, will always be that I lost some important years, and I will never get them back.

If you, too, have a strong-willed child, the good news is that it can be different for you and your child. By learning to adapt your parenting style, you can raise a child who is responsible; a child who is accountable for his or her actions; a child who respects others; a child who "catches" and keeps your values; and most important, a child who stays on point, on God's path—at least most of the time! And by adapting your parenting style to meet the needs of your strong-willed child, you can keep your child on this path without crushing his or her spirit.

Start today by making a commitment to learn as much as you can about the strong-willed child. Three good resources are James Dobson's books *The Strong-Willed Child* and *Parenting Isn't for Cowards*, and Cynthia Ulrich Tobias's *"You Can't Make Me" (But I Can Be Persuaded)*. Ms. Tobias, founder of Learning Styles Unlimited, Inc., was a strong-willed child herself and is now raising one. In her book she explains that strong-willed children are not being disobedient just because they want to do things their way. These children actually see the world differently. Here are a few helpful insights from her book.

PARENT POINT

Understanding the Strong-Willed Child

The Strong-Willed Child (SWC) . . .

- almost never accepts words like "impossible" or phrases like "it can't be done."

- can move with lightning speed from being a warm, loving presence to being a cold, immovable force.

- may argue the point into the ground, sometimes just to see how far into the ground the point will go.

- when bored, has been known to create a crisis rather than have a day go by without incident.

- considers rules to be more like guidelines (i.e., "As long as I'm abiding by the 'spirit of the law,' why are you being so picky?").

- shows great creativity and resourcefulness—seems to always find a way to accomplish a goal.
- can turn what seems to be the smallest issue into a grand crusade or a raging controversy.
- doesn't do things just because "you're supposed to"—it needs to matter personally.
- refuses to obey unconditionally—seems to always have a few terms of negotiation before complying.
- is not afraid to try the unknown—to conquer the unfamiliar (although each SWC chooses his or her own risks, they all seem to possess the confidence to try new things).
- can take what was meant to be the simplest request and interpret it as an offensive ultimatum.
- may not actually apologize but almost always makes things right.

—From *"You Can't Make Me" (But I Can Be Persuaded)*, by Cynthia Ulrich Tobias, pp. 9-10.

Let me end our description of the strong-willed child with an important point of clarification. Although negotiating or compromising is a key process in dealing with your strong-willed child, be sure you never negotiate or compromise your core values. If you do, you'll be on your way to creating the third type of child.

The Rebel

The third type of child is the rebel. A rebel can be a strong-willed child or a compliant child who rebels against the family values *and never comes back to them*. I have observed that 5 to 10 percent of the children I teach are rebels. Teachers generally say there are approximately one or two rebels in each class. Children become rebels in one of three ways.

Some children become rebels because there is no *recognizable* family value or belief system—no "North Star"—to guide them. As Stephen Covey suggests, the family value system should resemble a solid, three-dimensional cube—one that has depth and breadth and is built on a solid foundation. Unfortunately, the value system of many families is more like a skinny, one-dimensional ruler. A one-dimensional value system, which does not have a solid foundation, will not survive the many challenges of life.

I like to use the story of the three little pigs to drive the point home. We need a value system made of bricks, not one made of straw or sticks. Parents may claim to have an unspoken or "understood" family value system, yet those values are like "straw" or "sticks" if they are not communicated or supported adequately. Many families never clearly define their core values, many families never write a family mission statement, and many families never make important commitments such as keeping the family a high priority. Worst of all, many parents fail to model their values. Consequently, strong-willed children who live in houses built of straw or sticks never know when they are off point. When the big bad wolf blows (the artificial star), the house crumbles. The children are now on a new path, and there is nothing but the police to put them back on point.

In their book *Parenting with Love and Logic,* Cline and Fay explain that another way to create a rebel is to fail to understand how to raise a strong-willed child. Remember the theory of the upside down triangle? As a child grows, we give him or her more and more "space"—increasing the responsibilities, privileges, and freedoms while decreasing the limits and boundaries. Though this parenting approach is easy with a compliant child, it is more difficult with a strong-willed child. Often we get frustrated with the strong-willed child at an early age and, consequently, give way too much "space" way too soon. Then one day, when the child is older, we realize that we don't like the child who is standing before us. To correct the situation, we invert the triangle and start restricting the "space" (increasing the limits and boundaries) just at the age when the child needs more "space" (more responsibilities, privileges, and freedoms). At some point the child rebels against the tightening of limits and boundaries and rejects us, no longer trusting us. The child "turns us off," and we don't know why. Beth was heading in that direction before Curt died. Thankfully, after Curt's death I realized that Beth was all that I had left. I decided to change. I decided to build a strong relationship with her. I decided to offer her unconditional love. I can't say that I did all of these things properly, but I can say that I have never stopped trying.

I believe there is one more way to create a rebel. Let's say that you have a compliant son. By his sixteenth birthday, he has earned your trust by staying on point most of the time. However, you aren't seeing the world clearly because, as Stephen Covey says, you're looking at the world through your own pair of glasses—or, as I've come to call them, your own pair of sunglasses. In other words, you're seeing the world through your own life experiences, which "shade" or color your perception of the way things are. Instead, you should be looking through your child's glasses, or seeing things through your child's eyes. You remember what you were like when you were sixteen, and you know what you would have done if you had had a lot of freedom. So, in order to be at peace, you put unreasonable restrictions on your son. Your son rebels. What choice did he have? He played by the rules. He followed the family star and made your values his own. He thought he had earned your trust, but you acted as if you had reason not to trust him. Compliant children need to know that their "on point" behavior will continue to generate more privileges and freedoms the older they get. If we fail to allow them to grow, we run the risk of causing them to rebel.

Although even compliant children can become rebels, the majority of children who rebel are strong-willed children. Raising a strong-willed child, however, does not have to be a losing proposition! In fact, your strong-willed child actually places an incredible amount of importance on the relationship he or she has with you and needs to know that your love is truly unconditional. Therefore, maintaining a strong relationship with your strong-willed child is essential. Unfortunately, many parents believe that as their children get older, they won't have to spend as much time and energy parenting those children. I have found it to be just the opposite—especially with a strong-willed child. Though sometimes the rebellion that rears its ugly head is short-term, rebellion generally tends to surface in the preteen and teen years. This is one reason why parents need to spend more time with their children as they age, not less. Parents also need to help their children find adult role models who share the family's values. Caring adult relationships in the life of a strong-willed child are crucial for success. Once these relationships are cemented, then appropriate limits, boundaries, and consequences are very effective in helping to prevent the strong-willed child from becoming a rebel. Strong relationships in combination with effective limits and consequences, then, are the key elements that keep the strong-willed child on point. We will cover these important elements at length in section 2.

Please, please, please learn to adapt your parenting style for each child based on that child's personality, or temperament, and needs. You can do this without compromising your core family values. And if you do, you're much less likely to create a rebel later on.

Stay on Board!

Once parents begin to understand their children, they often become frustrated when their children don't "fit the mold" all the time. Remember that no one exhibits the same behavior all the time; we all assume different personalities at times. Don't give up the ship! Stay on board with me through section 2, and we will consider how you can help your children stay on point despite the differences and even the inconsistencies in their behavior.

Recently, I was interviewed by a local television station for a series of six-minute parenting segments. The interviewer was a mother of young children, so she had a vested interest in the interviews. The very first topic she mentioned was how to raise responsible children. Of all the reasons parents take my courses, again and again the number one reason is to learn how to raise responsible children. Now that we've laid the foundation, so to speak, it's time to build the house.

My mother-in-law is an active volunteer for Habitat for Humanity, and she often talks about the concept of "sweat equity." Each future homeowner must put in a certain number of hours, helping to build the house. Likewise, every parent must put in many, many hours in order to build a house that will withstand all the evils that live outside. Section 2 will enable you to reap huge dividends for your time and effort. It will give you some important "how-to's" for raising both the compliant and the strong-willed child. More important, it will help you to keep

God's love in the forefront of your parenting and significantly increase the possibility that your child will be a loving child—a child who feels the love of God each and every day, a child who is responsible for his or her actions, and a child who will stay on point.

QUESTIONS TO PONDER

1. Although no child is 100 percent compliant or strong-willed, which type best describes each of your children? How do you need to tailor your parenting approach in order to meet the needs of each child?

2. Are you following the upside-down triangle parenting method?

3. Are you consistently rewarding your compliant child with increasing responsibilities and freedoms?

4. Are you willing to compromise with your strong-willed child in areas that do not involve core values?

5. Do you show your children that you celebrate their differences? If you have only one child, how do you show this child that you celebrate his or her unique characteristics and personality traits?

RAISING RESPONSIBLE CHILDREN

The righteous walk in integrity—
happy are the children who follow them!

—*Proverbs 20:7*

4

EMPOWERING YOUR CHILDREN

Scripture Link

For we are each responsible for our own conduct.
—*Galatians 6:5 NLT*

Teach [your children] to exercise self-control, to be worthy of respect, and to live wisely. They must have strong faith and be filled with love and patience. . . . And you yourself must be an example to them.
—*Titus 2:2, 7 NLT*

Have you ever listened to parents explain why their children have flunked out of college? One parent told me that her college-age child could not get out of bed in time to make it to class. The child expected the dorm to be a hotel and was dismayed to find out that the dorm did not have morning wake-up call service. The child then relied on the roommate, but many times the roommate would forget or would sleep in as well. Another parent told me that his child could not make the right choice concerning whether to go to a night class or attend choir practice for the fraternity. Both of these "children" were almost adults themselves, yet they had not learned to practice responsibility.

Most parents would agree that one of their primary tasks is to teach their children to be responsible, yet so many children never learn this essential life skill. Many times my parenting classes include elementary school teachers. When I talk about the need for children to be responsible for doing their own homework and school projects, they stand up and cheer. The teachers particularly enjoy this rhetorical question: Did you know that a child could flunk a fifth-grade science project and still go to college? The point is this: If we want to teach our children responsibility, then we must be willing to allow them to make mistakes—and, yes, even fail.

Enabling Leads to Irresponsibility and Inability

When I started teaching parenting courses, I became familiar with the Hazelden company, an organization that has created numerous videos and pamphlets on issues relating to children and parents. The first thing I learned from Hazelden was the difference between enabling and empowering. Enabling is the process of never letting our children learn from their mistakes. Empowering is the exact opposite: allowing our children to learn from their mistakes. Before exploring how we can empower our children, it's helpful to consider some of the ways we enable our children.

Parenting with Love and Logic, which I introduced in the previous chapter, is one of the best books I have read on the subject of teaching our children to be responsible. In this book, Cline and Fay describe two ineffective parenting styles, or personalities, that enable children and prevent them from learning responsibility. It has been my observation that whenever we parents enable our children, we generally assume one of these two personalities. Sometimes we become the "drill sergeant parent." We snap out orders, never giving our children the opportunity to make a decision for themselves. Many experts claim that when we do this, our children start to doubt their own abilities. Other times we become the "helicopter parent." We hover over our children, just waiting for them to be in a situation where a difficult decision has to be made. Just when they are ready to take some action, we swoop down and make the decision for them. Or when we see our children facing a problem, we fire missiles from our high-powered helicopters and destroy the problem.

Despite our well-intentioned efforts to protect our children, whether by giving orders or by saving the day, we set our children up for failure when we enable them. Ironically, failure is exactly what many of us are trying to help our children avoid in the first place!

Enabling is a disease of epidemic proportions these days.

Though it's especially prevalent among overly protective parents, who may have a fear of failure, and highly successful parents, who may be unaccustomed to failure and have a low tolerance for it, we're all "infected" with the disease at one time or another. Unfortunately, it's our children who suffer the harmful effects of the disease. We don't want our children to fail, so we tell them how to solve the problem or do the task, or we simply do it for them ourselves. Yet even if we enable our children to succeed at the task at hand, our enabling ultimately prevents them from learning how to think for themselves, solve problems, and overcome challenges—vital skills for life in the "real world." Our enabling also prevents them from learning the value of always giving your best effort. And when children are rewarded without giving their best effort, they begin to think, "If I don't do it, they will," thus perpetuating the disease. Certainly we don't enjoy seeing our children unhappy; we don't enjoy seeing our children facing a difficult decision; and we don't enjoy seeing our children fail. Yet we must remember that such experiences, though painful, are essential learning opportunities for our children.

One of the most common learning opportunities enabling parents "steal" from their children is the class project. I once was in a teacher's office when a parent called to ask the teacher a question about the project that the parent was doing for the child. After hanging up the phone, the teacher exclaimed that some parents have no shame! Regrettably, it's not an isolated incident. Too often the typical class project becomes the parent's project, rather than the child's, because the parent's reputation is on the line—or so the parent thinks. The parent assumes that if the child gets a bad grade, it will be a bad reflection on the parent. Over the last several years I have come to realize that this attitude is often prevalent in high-income parents who are successful in the business world and want their children to be successful as well.

Though the enabling disease is widespread, there is hope. There is an antidote, and it's called empowering.

Empowering Leads to Responsibility and Capability

When we empower our children, we help them to become both responsible and capable. Though empowering is essentially allowing our children to learn from their mistakes, it involves other important life lessons as well. Two particularly important life lessons we teach our children when we empower them are problem solving and resiliency.

Problem solving is a life lesson that I find many children have not learned. My own parents' approach to school projects allowed me to learn this valuable skill. When I was a child, my dad never helped me with school projects. I was never sure whether he was lazy or just an empowering parent. Looking back, I now know that he was empowering me! I usually could count on my mom for a little bit of help—at least until it came time for the class project in physics my senior year. When I announced that I had to do a physics project on motion, my mom told me that she had no mechanical capabilities, and my dad, as usual, told me to have fun. "Oh, no!" I exclaimed. "I can't possibly do a project on motion!" Then I had a great idea that would solve my problem. My uncle Flip loved working with his hands, and he had a great workbench. Uncle Flip didn't have a son, so I was like a son to him. When I asked him to help me, he was very excited about the project. Together we designed a wonderful project on motion. When I left his house, I knew that my project was in good hands. For several weeks I left my uncle alone so that he could work at his own pace.

Occasionally I would check in with my uncle, and he would assure me that things were going well. The Friday before the Monday when the project was due, I drove to his house. I asked my aunt how the project was going, and she said those awful words that I will always remember: "What project?" I ran down into the basement and saw the drawings still lying on the workbench. "Where is Uncle Flip?" I screamed. "He's away on a business trip," my aunt responded. "Ugh!"

There I sat in a pool of pitiful tears. I had one weekend to finish the biggest project of the year, and there was no one to blame but myself. I got myself off the basement floor and began to problem-solve the situation. I knew how to hammer a nail, I knew how to drill a hole, and I knew how to saw a piece of wood. My uncle's shop had a lot of wood, a hammer, a saw, and a drill. All I needed was a project idea on motion. The only idea that came to mind was a game my little sister had called "Mousetrap."

I spent Saturday and Sunday making a similar game out of

wood. I did have to "borrow" one of the plastic mice from my sister's game. The motion was created with a marble. You dropped the marble into a hole, and it ran down a series of wooden rails. Finally the marble reached the bottom, where it hit a pencil that had been glued in an upward position. Positioned on top of the pencil was a small paper cup. When the pencil vibrated, the cup fell and captured the mouse. When the project was done, I stained and varnished the wood. Needless to say, I didn't get a very good night's sleep on Sunday.

From Monday to Thursday, our teacher—let's call him Mr. Newton—reviewed each project after school. On Friday, he would present the top three projects. I had trouble eating breakfast Friday morning because I knew we were getting our grades that day. When I got to class, a sheet covered each project; but I still knew that I had the worst project of them all. My only unanswered question was whether I was going to get a D or an F. Although my parents always held us accountable for our efforts and never belittled my grades, I had never brought home a D or an F.

"Okay, class, let's start looking at the top projects," Mr. Newton said. "Mr. Williams, please come to the front of the room and demonstrate your project."

Now, Mr. Newton was a tough teacher, but he was a fair and kind man; and it seemed to me that this masochistic behavior was totally out of character! I just sat there, frozen to my chair. "Mr. Williams, please come to the front of the class and demonstrate your project," he repeated. I dutifully went to the front of the room. I got my project and stood it on his desk. I then removed the sheet. I wish I could describe the expressions on my classmates' faces. Some showed pity, some showed delight, and some were hidden in their hands. Initially, there was a hush, and then, slowly, there were a few laughs and giggles. "Come on, Mr. Williams, show the class how this works. I love this project!" Mr. Newton exclaimed.

After demonstrating my mousetrap and listening to the snickering from my classmates, I couldn't believe what happened next. Mr. Newton told me that I had gotten a B. Did I hear a D? No, he said I got a *B*. He went on to say in front of the whole class that my project was the only one that he was 100 percent sure had been done without any help.

Regardless of my good grade, I learned some valuable lessons.

For one thing, I learned that I was capable of solving a difficult problem all by myself. I also learned that it's more difficult to solve problems when we put things off to the last minute. Finally, I learned that when we solve problems by ourselves, we feel a great sense of satisfaction and pride. These important lessons helped me develop the skill of problem solving, which I would use in college as well as throughout the rest of my life.

Resiliency is another important life lesson that all children need to learn, especially in today's rapidly changing, volatile world. Though children develop resiliency in many ways, perhaps the most important way is through empowerment. I always think of Beth when I think of resiliency.

One afternoon a camera crew and hostess came to the house. They walked throughout the family room looking at all of the pictures. The reporter already knew that we had lost Curt years earlier, and that recently we had lost Beth's fiancé, our future son-in-law. She wanted the first segment to be about the pictures and Beth's life. "How does she keep going?" the reporter asked. I responded by saying that Beth is the most resilient person I have ever known.

Beth developed resiliency because we allowed her to learn from her mistakes. She suffered disappointments from a very young age, and she learned how to deal with them. As a result, she learned how to brush herself off and "get back on the horse."

Unfortunately, many children never develop resiliency. Experts claim that one of the main reasons why the United States has such a high teen suicide rate is that our young people are not resilient. I will always remember the time when one of Curt's high school classmates committed suicide. He had just broken up with his girlfriend. He came home, said goodnight to his parents, and waited for them to go to sleep. He then went down to the garage and started the car. His parents found him the next morning. How tragic. Our young people today desperately need us to teach them how to be resilient. They need us to teach them how to think positively and do their best. They need us to teach them how to persevere and make the best of difficult situations. They need us to teach them how to handle life's disappointments and tragedies. They need us to teach them to trust in God and believe God can help them solve their problems. They need us to teach them how to make sound, moral decisions (if we help them learn and understand God's teachings, they will always know whether their choices are the right ones). All of these are ways we can help our children develop resiliency.

Yes, we teach our children important life lessons—lessons that help them to become responsible and capable—when we empower them. We empower our children when we allow them to solve their own problems. We empower our children when we help them develop resiliency. We empower our children when we encourage them to make their own choices and let them learn from their mistakes. We empower our children when we expect them to do their own work. We empower our children when we allow them to show their independence. We empower our children when we teach them about God and nurture their faith. Empowerment builds character. Enabling destroys character. The choice is ours.

Four Practical Ways to Empower Your Child

1. Allow your children to assume responsibility for morning and bedtime routines as age permits.

Learning is a gradual and progressive process. We begin with the basics and progress to more advanced concepts. The same is true of learning responsibility. We begin with simple tasks and progress to more complex tasks as we demonstrate our competence and dependability. As parents, we can empower our children from a very young age by teaching them to assume more and more responsibility for basic personal tasks and routines. Among other things, toddlers and preschoolers can learn to master potty training, brushing their teeth, combing their hair, and making choices of what to wear and eat, and helping to dress and undress themselves. Then, when they're ready to start school, they're also ready to assume the kind of responsibilities appropriate for school-age children.

If you have school-age children, I suggest you buy an alarm clock for each child. I also recommend you not spend much money because these clocks may "take flight" from time to time! One way to prevent "flying clocks" and also ensure that your child actually gets out of the bed is to put the clock on a dresser or bookshelf away from the bed, requiring the child to get up to turn off the clock. Once you tell your children that they now have the responsibility of waking themselves up in the morning, you must sit back and watch. If the child turns off the clock and goes back to sleep, then a consequence should follow. Obviously, if you have your own schedule to keep and cannot afford to be late, then the consequence will have to be something such as losing a privilege. However, if you don't have a pressing schedule, then the child can receive the natural consequence that comes from being late to school. (I will cover consequences in greater detail in chapter 6, including what to do if the child continues to oversleep.) Parents continue to tell me that the alarm clock does wonders for family harmony. Children are so proud of their new responsibility, especially when their parents give them positive reinforcement each and every morning. It helps to get everyone's morning off to a good start!

Another suggestion is to have your school-age children choose what they will wear and get the clothes ready the night before they need them. Many parents empower their children even more by allowing them to wear any clothes they want as long as the clothes are clean and meet the school's dress code. As little as it may seem, this simple choice goes a long way toward building children's self-esteem, confidence, and sense of responsibility.

In addition to getting themselves up and dressed for the day, school-age children may be expected to gather all their books, homework assignments, and other items needed for the day, including lunch or lunch money. (Of course, kindergartners, who are new to the school routine, will need some assistance.) Some parents even allow their children to make their own lunches (either the night before or, time permitting, in the morning), as they are ready to do so. Other parents also expect their children to complete a few household chores—such as making the bed, feeding a pet, or taking out the trash—before leaving for school or going to bed.

All of these simple tasks can do wonders to empower your children. The rewards for your children are not monetary or material but intrinsic in nature, coming from your expressions of gratitude and praise. Yet, remember that it is parental approval children desire the most. On occasion, of course, your family may choose to go to a favorite eating establishment to celebrate these important steps toward responsibility. Your rewards are twofold: seeing your children take on new responsibilities and enjoying a more pleasant atmosphere in the home, which results as your children's responsibilities increase and frustration, anger, and conflict significantly decrease. This type of parenting is a win/win proposition!

2. Teach your school-age children to assume responsibility for all their assignments and projects.

As mentioned previously, we empower our children when we allow them to assume responsibility for their own schoolwork, including special assignments and projects. Parents often ask me, "When is it okay to help my children?" Although this is often a juggling act, here are some helpful guidelines.

First of all, talk with your child's teacher early in the year to determine his or her position on parental assistance with homework and other projects. In most cases, helping your child understand an assignment or work through a question or problem should be fine. If, however, you feel your child does not have the proper skills necessary to complete the homework or project, I recommend you talk to the teacher. Teachers often tell me how difficult it can be to determine whether their methods are falling short if parents are always correcting or completing their children's homework.

When it comes to special projects, your primary role should be to assist your child with planning and organization. To determine how much help your child needs in these areas, ask him or her to identify the steps necessary for completing the project, the amount of time required for each step, and the needed supplies. I recommend you buy a small, magnetic wipe-off board that can be attached to the refrigerator door to help keep your child "on track." Let me explain how this works by presenting the classic case of Joey's science project—first with enabling parents, and then with empowering parents.

Joey is in the fifth grade. His science project is to begin on September 15 and end on October 15. His enabling parents want to stay on top of the project the entire four weeks. Every day Joey is to set aside time for the project. Every night Joey is to give his parents an update. Dad helps Joey design the project. Mom helps Joey do the project. Even so, sometimes Joey gets behind; and his parents respond, "You are grounded, Joey, until the project is done." For four weeks, their home is full of anger and distrust. For four weeks, Joey doesn't feel any sense of accomplishment.

Now let's consider the approach that would be taken by empowering parents. Joey's parents write the project and it's beginning and ending dates on the wipe-off board. They have Joey describe the project to them. Then they tell Joey that he needs to decide what supplies he will need. They agree to get the supplies during the first week. They also agree that if Joey lacks certain skills to do the project, they will teach Joey those skills during the first week. They commit to take Joey to the library during the first three weeks of the project, but he must give them advance notice of when the trips will be necessary. They do not nag Joey about the project or ask for a status report. Joey takes full responsibility for completing the project. As the project progresses, they evaluate whether or not Joey is giving his best effort. He knows that there will be negative consequences waiting for him if he does not give the project his best effort. When Joey gets his grade, he is the sole owner of that grade. And if his parents feel he did his best, regardless of the grade received, Joey gets many words of praise. They know that at this point in his life, grades are secondary to the important life skill of learning how to plan and complete a project on time.

By the way, you can use the magnetic project board as a personal message center for your child whenever a special project is not underway. Write positive or encouraging messages such as "I love you" or "We're proud of you." Some parents buy a project/message board for each child. In any case, it's a great way to help children manage their own assignments and projects.

3. Allow your children to grow in independence.

Independence is inevitable. From the minute they are born, our children are on a journey toward independence. Our job as parents is to prepare them for full independence by allowing them to grow in independence through the years. Oftentimes, children who are not allowed to grow in independence wind up being off point. They think that choosing to follow their parents' star, or values, wouldn't really be a choice at all. In fact, they will even make a bad choice just to depart from their parents' values and show their independence. This is why it is so important for us not only to help our children "catch" our values and accept them as their own, but also to allow them to make their own choices and grow in independence.

When our children are young, we can help them gain a sense of independence by giving them the power to choose between two alternatives. Of course, one of these alternatives should reflect the family's values, or North Star. If they make a wrong or poor

choice, we should be willing to allow them to suffer the consequences of that choice (again, we'll discuss consequences in detail
in chapter 6). Then, as they begin to make wise choices and earn
our trust, we should be willing to give them more independence—
in other words, more "space" and more freedom to choose.
Independence is linked to trust, which is earned. However, as we
discussed previously, we run the risk of creating rebels when we do
not reward our children's trustworthiness with increased independence. We can feel comfortable allowing our children to grow
in independence if we have a solid relationship with them.
Relationships, after all, are the key to effective parenting.

Although empowering our children by allowing them to grow in
independence doesn't ensure that they won't make mistakes when
they are older, it does significantly improve the probability. As our
children recognize that we have confidence in their choices, they
become more confident and secure themselves and, therefore, more
willing to follow our values and accept them as their own.

**Please, please, please build confidence in your children by allow-
ing them to grow in independence. Allow your children to learn
from their mistakes when they are young and the consequences are
much less serious than those of mistakes such as drunk driving,
doing drugs, or having premarital sex.**

4. Nurture your children's faith.

When we empower our children, we give them the freedom to
make their own choices and solve their own problems. As parents,
we can increase the probability that our children will make the
"right" choices and decisions by nurturing their faith. Faith
empowers our children to do the right thing (instead of what feels
good), make wise decisions, act responsibly, solve problems, handle life's disappointments and tragedies, and live abundant, hope-
ful lives. As we will see in chapter 10, one of the most important
ways we nurture our children and their faith is through our own
expressions of love. Oftentimes, however, we stop there, leaving
the remaining development of our children's faith to the professionals—the church professionals, that is. But the truth is, no one
has more influence in our children's spiritual lives than we do as
parents. If we really want to nurture our children's faith, then we

must be involved in their spiritual development on a daily basis. We must do as Deuteronomy 6:7 instructs and make our faith a part of our daily lives, talking about it "when [we] sit at home and when [we] walk along the road, when [we] lie down and when [we] get up" (NIV). There are entire books devoted to this subject, and I highly recommend you consult the experts for specific guidance. For now, however, here are a few basics to consider.

PARENT POINT
Everyday Ways to Nurture Your Children's Faith

1. Make yours a home where faith is both taught and "caught." Talk openly and frequently about your own faith and live out or model your beliefs for your children.

2. Pray together—not only at meals but at other times as well. If you begin the nightly ritual of praying together when your child is young, you will feel comfortable continuing this practice into the difficult teen years.

3. Have a regular family devotion time. Read the Bible together and discuss how biblical principles apply to life today, including specific situations in your own lives. (There are many excellent family devotional resources available.)

4. Allow everyday moments to become opportunities for acknowledging God's presence and making faith connections (e.g., thanking God for a beautiful sunset, pointing out how God provided strength or help in a particular situation, talking about the day's blessings while eating dinner together, and so forth).

5. Make church involvement a high family priority.

6. Make yours a home where faith is both taught and "caught." Talk openly and frequently about your own faith and live out or model your beliefs for your children.

QUESTIONS TO PONDER

1. Do you sometimes find yourself being a helicopter parent and/or a drill sergeant parent? What steps can you take to keep from enabling your children?

2. What are the key differences between being an enabling parent and an empowering parent? In what ways do you enable your children? In what ways do you empower your children? What else can you do to empower your children?

3. Have you given your children sufficient opportunities to learn how to solve problems? What can you do to help them develop this important life skill?

4. How often do you talk to your children's teachers? Do you know each teacher's viewpoint concerning your involvement with homework and class projects?

5. Do you believe your children are resilient? What evidence supports your view? What can you do to help your children become more resilient?

6. Are you allowing your children to grow in their independence? What can you do to help them prepare for and earn this privilege?

7. How are you nurturing your children's faith? What else can you do to encourage their faith development and spiritual growth?

5

SETTING LIMITS AND BOUNDARIES

Scripture Link

My child, keep your father's commandment,
and do not forsake your mother's teaching.
Bind them upon your heart always;
tie them around your neck.
When you walk, they will lead you;
when you lie down, they will watch over you;
and when you awake, they will talk with you.
                                    —Proverbs 6:20-22

Whoever can be trusted with very little can also be
trusted with much.   *—Luke 16:10a NIV*

Our goal is to stay within the boundaries of God's plan
for us.   *—2 Corinthians 10:13b NLT*

Once we have found the courage to empower our children, we must implement limits and boundaries in their lives. Although empowering our children means we allow them to make more decisions and learn from their mistakes, it does not mean we give them unlimited freedom. Children need appropriate limits and boundaries in their lives. As Dr. Jane Bluestein explains in her book *Parents, Teens, and Boundaries*, "Boundaries are anything marking a limit and are essential for all healthy relationships. They represent the conditions under which we [parents] will participate, or continue to participate, in some activity" (p. 4).

When discussing limits and boundaries, I always ask two questions. First, do you enjoy uncertainty in your life? Most of us do not. You see, uncertainty leads to insecurity, and we don't want to feel insecure. Children are no different. One of the most basic needs a child has is to feel secure. Limits and boundaries help to provide that security while allowing our children to become more responsible.

Second, do you know any children who don't respect the law? Most of us do. All children, even the strong-willed ones, need to know when they have stepped over the line. All children need to learn to respect the laws that govern our world. As experts confirm, children who learn to respect limits and boundaries learn to respect the law as well. Likewise, all children need to be held accountable for certain responsibilities. As a child's behavior demonstrates that he or she can handle additional responsibilities, then it's time to expand the child's limits and boundaries. Recall the upside down triangle we discussed in chapter 3 (see p. 54 to review). As children approach the end of their high school career, they need to be able to make decisions—both easy ones and difficult ones—without our help. By appropriately decreasing our children's limits and boundaries as they get older, we help to make their transition into adulthood more successful.

Limits and boundaries, then, give our children security while preparing them to become responsible adults.

Four Key Characteristics

Effective limits and boundaries require careful thought and study. They cannot simply be created "on the fly." Various experts agree that effective limits and boundaries must have several key characteristics: they must be clearly stated, they must be reasonable, they must be communicated in advance, and they must be age-appropriate and based on current behavior patterns. Let's consider each of these in more depth.

1. Limits and boundaries must be clearly stated.

Here is an example of an unclear limit. "Joey, you have to come home after the game is over." So, after the game Joey joins his friends at the local pizza place and then goes home. Joey says, "Mom, you didn't tell me *when* after the game I had to come home!" Can't you just see the hair standing up on Mom's neck? To set a clear limit, she might have told Joey to be home thirty minutes after the game was over, or she might have told him to be home by a specific time.

A good way to determine whether or not the limits and boundaries you have set for your children are clear is to "run them past your children." I suggest you write a list of limits and boundaries on a piece of paper. Be sure to write a separate list for each child if there are significant gaps in age or differences in expectations. Then read the list(s) to your children and have them repeat each limit and tell what it means. If they are able to do this, then the limit is clear. If not, work on the wording together until your children have complete understanding.

2. Limits and boundaries must be reasonable.

"It's not fair!" Sound familiar? Because our children often say this to express their displeasure when they don't get their own way, we tend to ignore the comment even when our children are protesting an unfair limit or boundary. The truth is, sometimes we parents do set limits and boundaries that are unreasonable; and when we do, our children view them as punishment. Punishment should never be our objective because, as Dr. Fitzhugh Dodson explains, it "often has the effect of teaching the child to behave in exactly the opposite way from the way we want him to behave!" (*How to Father*). Many parents use punishment, he suggests, simply because they have never learned more effective ways to discipline their children. I have found that just as God's limits for us are grounded in love and wisdom, so also the limits we set for our children must be grounded in love and wisdom. As a result, unconditional love, rather than anger, will become contagious in our homes.

Parents frequently ask me how to know if a limit is reasonable or unreasonable. Let me offer three suggestions. First of all, never set a limit when you are angry. As Dr. Tim Kimmel, a minister by training, states in his video parenting course *Raising Children Who Turn Out Right: A Practical Strategy for Positive Parenting*, limits that are set when there is no anger in your heart will probably be reasonable. (The same rule of thumb works well when determining reasonable consequences, which we will discuss in chapter 6.) Second, be sure that the limit does not compromise any of your family's core values. A reasonable limit is one that upholds or reinforces your core values. Finally, if you're in doubt, talk to other parents whose values are in line with yours—perhaps the parents of your children's close friends. Obviously, if their values oppose yours, then a comparison does not make sense. If you are blessed by having relationships with other parents who share your values, maintain a constant dialogue with them—not only about limits and boundaries, but about other parenting issues as well. In addition to casual conversation, I recommend you meet together at least once a quarter to share your experiences and ideas. Let's say that you have a fifth grader who has several classmates who live in your neighborhood. In the summertime, you allow her to play outside with her friends until 7:00 P.M. One night after coming in on time, she asks if her curfew may be changed to 8:00 P.M. She says that all the other parents allow their children to play outside until then, and it's still light at that time during the summer. What should you do? First of all, you know that now is an acceptable time to make a decision because you're not angry or upset for any reason. Second, you know from prior conversations with parents in the neighborhood that they do allow their children to stay out until 8:00 P.M. Finally, you conclude that extending the curfew one hour in the summertime won't compromise any of your family's core values, including safety. It is a reasonable limit.

Ironically, it is often our best intentions that lead to unreasonable limits. One mom told me that after learning how much time most children spend watching television, she decided to get rid of all of the televisions in the house. She was very proud of herself. I asked her one simple question: "Where did your children spend their time last week after school?" After thinking for a minute, she realized that they had spent the entire afternoon at the house next door. She decided that she would rather them be at home, so she went out the next day and bought a television. This time, however, she put specific and reasonable boundaries in place concerning the amount of time and the types of shows the children were allowed to watch. She also spent time watching some of these approved shows *with* her children. She learned an important lesson: Limits must be reasonable in order to be effective.

3. Limits and boundaries must be communicated in advance.

Advance notice is another must for effective limits and boundaries. It's unfair to give a child a consequence for an unstated limit or boundary, or to tell a child at the last minute that he or she is not allowed to participate in a particular activity. Communicating limits and boundaries in advance not only helps our children to meet our expectations, but also to feel that we have a sense of fairness and goodwill toward them.

Of course, sometimes our children forget what we've told them they can and cannot do, and sometimes they have a different understanding or interpretation of a particular limit or boundary. For example, Joey and his parents were having a disagreement about whether or not he would be going to a party his friends were having Friday night. "Joey, we told you that you could never go to a party that was not chaperoned," his parents reminded him. "But *everyone* is going," Joey pleaded, "and I don't remember you saying *'never'*!" This is why it's wise to post a list of "rules" in a high-traffic area, such as on the refrigerator door or in the child's room. With younger children, reviewing and repeating the rules regularly together works equally well.

When it comes to actually writing your list(s) of limits and boundaries, adopt the KISS principle: Keep It Simple, Stupid! In other words, if your list resembles the Dead Sea Scrolls, then it's too long! Include only those items that need attention. For example, if your child is not having trouble coming home by curfew, then it isn't really necessary to include this on the written list. Also, it's better not to create the list by yourself. Have your child assist you. As you review the rules together, you will be able to ensure that each one is both clear and reasonable.

4. Limits and boundaries must be age appropriate and based on current behavior patterns.

All children want limits to be based on *future* behavior patterns. "Dad, if you let me stay out one hour later, I promise that I will always be home on time." Right! Limits and boundaries should never be based on children's future behavior patterns or promised behavior changes. Instead, their age and current behavior patterns—which demonstrate their level of maturity and responsibility—should be the determining factors.

As the second-born in my family, I always wanted the same curfews and other privileges that my older brother had. But despite my yearnings, I knew that in order for my limits and boundaries to expand, my behavior had to demonstrate that I was becoming more responsible, more accountable, and more dependable. In other words, I had to prove to my parents that I was trustworthy. Of course, I knew there were some limits that wouldn't change until I reached a certain age. When I reached the magical age of sixteen and received my driver's license, for example, my limits and freedoms expanded tremendously. In addition to being able to drive, I was pleasantly surprised when my curfew was extended to midnight. According to Pennsylvania state law, that was the hour when all sixteen-year-olds had to be off the road. State law also stated that upon turning seventeen, a driver was eligible to be treated as an adult—in other words, no curfew—if that driver had passed a driver's education course and had received no tickets. Needless to say, I never missed the midnight curfew!

Because I earned my parents' trust during my first year of driving, I was given the opportunity to spread my wings even more. During my senior year, my parents gave me permission to drive my mom's car to my brother's college four hours away. My best friend, Howdy, went with me. Both Howdy and I felt that this was a test, and we weren't going to do anything to fail it! Because I was going for an interview, my high school excused us from attending school that Friday. We arrived safely, and I was on time for my interview. Then, after spending the weekend with my brother and his fraternity brothers, we drove safely home on Sunday. I'm not sure who was prouder—our parents or the two of us!

If your firstborn accepts limits with little fanfare and your second-born tends to fight limits, then you might find it helpful to follow the suggestion I made regarding strong-willed children: Take lots of home videos! That way, when the younger child asks for expanded limits based strictly on age, you can show the child videos of his or her behavior! After showing the movies and confirming past behavior, you can then explain to the child that when his or her behavior demonstrates the appropriate level of maturity and responsibility, you will be happy to expand his or her limits and privileges.

All Children Test the Limits

All children test the limits their parents have set for them. It's part of the human experience. As I've mentioned previously, strong-willed children, in particular, challenge the limits more often. Consequently, their parents often become tired and frustrated with their behavior and give in, expanding the limits too early. "The whining is driving me crazy!" they exclaim. Regardless of their children's temperaments, however, all parents must be strong and refuse to give in to their children if they want them to respect limits, including those set by society. As I've said previously, it's better for children to learn to respect limits while they're young and the consequences of violating those limits are less serious.

As a child, I never found it difficult to accept or live within the limits and boundaries my parents set. The limits never seemed unreasonable, even when I compared them to those of my friends. And as I got older, my freedom grew. But like any normal child, I, too, tested the limits my parents set. There is one story that my mom enjoys telling my daughter. One night just before I left the house to go to a dance at our church, my mother told me to change my pants. "These are my dancing pants!" I exclaimed. My mother proceeded to tell me that they were too tight around my behind, and that she was not going to have people at the church talking about her son's rear end. I thought she was kidding, so I kept walking out the door. "One more step, James Curtis, and you will not be going to the dance!" she called. Now, whenever my mom would call me by my proper name, I knew it was time to listen. So I went upstairs and changed my pants; but before I came back downstairs, I threw my green dancing pants out the window into the side yard. When I got outside, I changed my pants and went to the dance. *What she doesn't know won't hurt her,* I told myself.

Whenever I tried to out-fox my parents, I usually failed. This time was no exception. My mother taught nursery school at the church; and on the following Monday, the youth minister told her what a great dancer I was—especially in my tight green pants. Needless to say, I never saw those pants again!

As parents, we must accept the fact that all children will test limits from time to time. This is why it is so important for us to work with our children to develop limits and boundaries that are appropriate to their maturity level and sense of responsibility. Then, when our children complain about the limits that have been placed in their lives, we must "dig in" our heels and stand firm. We shouldn't expect a lot of hugs and kisses from our children for putting limits in their lives. Instead, we can hope for the day when our adult children will look back and offer gratitude for those limits, as many often do.

Chores Teach Responsibility

Parents often ask me why I include chores in the discussion of limits and boundaries. I jokingly say that I don't know where else to put them! Actually, the truth is that chores are closely related to limits and boundaries. Like limits and boundaries, chores are fundamental to the task of raising responsible children. Like limits and boundaries, they are a critical way to teach children how to demonstrate responsibility. And, like limits and boundaries, they can cause much grief and anger in the home if they are implemented improperly. Here are some suggestions to help you avoid potential problems.

PARENT POINT
Staying on Track with Chores

1. A chore should meet a family need. Chores should not be a "make work" project. When I was in the United States Navy, I spent hours completing "make work" projects. My resentment was very high. Likewise, children will resent doing chores that do not meet a family need.

2. Chores should be rotated among siblings whenever possible. This helps to compensate for the fact that some chores are mundane while others are more interesting or

---

exciting, especially if they get the children out of the house. Remember, however, that some chores can be dangerous if the child doesn't have the necessary maturity and skill level (e.g., mowing the lawn) and should be assigned accordingly.

3. As parents, it is our responsibility to teach our children the skills necessary for performing their chores.

4. Clarify that all family members are expected to do chores without being paid. It is a responsibility of being a family member. Only "special jobs" such as painting the backyard fence or cleaning the garage should earn our children money. (My dad would remind me that my mother didn't get paid for cooking. Likewise, my dad never got paid for doing the dishes night after night.) Explain, however, that there are numerous jobs children can perform outside of the home to earn money. (My brother and I shared the responsibility of cutting the grass and were not paid for this chore. However, both of us cut many of our neighbors' lawns for payment.)

5. Make sure that you are not expecting perfection, and always give lots of praise when chores are done. Expect strong-willed children to want to complete the task entirely different from the way you would complete the task! Even if the child's way takes longer and does not complete the task to your level of satisfaction, you should allow the child to have his or her way. (I know from my own experience with Beth that this is a battle not worth fighting.)

6. Set up a time frame for the completion of each chore, and hold your children accountable.

7. Be careful not to discriminate with chores. Don't have the boys do only yard work and the girls do only housework. Both boys and girls need to learn how to do the many responsibilities associated with running a house.

8. As children get older and their responsibilities outside the home increase (schoolwork, extracurricular activities, after-school jobs), it is advisable to reduce the number of chores they are required to do.

When I was growing up, I had a friend who didn't have any chores to do. "It's not fair!" I would complain. My dad would simply tell me that if my friend's parents were willing to raise me and pay for my food and clothing, then it was okay for me to live with them! It's an age-old problem: Children think that chores are unfair and that they do all the work. I once read of an easy way to handle this problem. Have a family meeting and work together to list on a piece of paper all the responsibilities that need to be accounted for in your home. Then, identify who is accountable for each responsibility and list that person's name beside the task. At the end of this process, your children should no longer complain that you aren't carrying your weight! Children who understand that chores are part of the family structure feel they are part of the family. Children who learn how to complete chores on time without a lot of nagging from their parents become dependable. In short, chores are an excellent way to teach children responsibility.

Please, please, please do not underestimate the value of having your children do chores.

It's Worth the Trouble

Generally speaking, children view limits and boundaries— including the requirement of doing chores—as restrictions on their behavior. To make matters worse, many times we do not write or present the limits correctly, causing our children to view them as punishment. Parents often tell me they have trouble justifying limits and boundaries to their children. They wonder if it's really worth all the trouble. The answer is "YES!" In fact, as Dr. Jane Bluestein points out, much of the conflict that occurs between parents and children can be traced back to a lack of boundaries (*Parents, Teens, and Boundaries*, p. 5).

A few years ago, we built a lake house that sits in the back of a long cove. We soon discovered that the cove was a favorite spot for kids to ride their wave runners. After watching the kids fly up and down the cove at such high speeds, endangering their lives, I decided to install a buoy that read: "Go slow, heavy congestion." I talked with several people to learn how to install a buoy. I discovered that in addition to the buoy, I would need to buy a large cement block and enough heavy chain to reach the bottom of the lake. Then I would attach the buoy to the chain, connect the chain to the cement block, and sink the block to the bottom of the lake. The procedure itself made a lot of sense to me. What surprised me was the *cost* of the procedure! Still, I recognized that without the cement block and the long, heavy, expensive chain, the buoy might blow away during storms or other turbulence. Suddenly the "light bulb" in my head lit up, and I realized that I had just found a parable that would help parents to understand and explain the need for limits and boundaries.

The buoy represents the limits and boundaries we set for our children. Like the buoy, limits and boundaries serve as helpful reminders and guideposts to keep our children safe from harm. The chain represents our family value or belief system, which is anchored to our faith—the cement block. Without the strong, secure connection to the chain and cement block, the buoy is easily blown away and lost during strong winds and storms. Likewise, when we take the easy approach and give in to our children, they don't survive the storms. But when we are careful to tie limits and boundaries to a strong, secure belief system—a belief system anchored to a foundation of faith—then our children will survive the many turbulent times that lie ahead. They may be blown and shaken, but they will survive!

The parable holds true for us as well, doesn't it? We, too, have limits and boundaries—limits and boundaries set for us by God. And if we observe these limits and boundaries, which are tied to the unshakable foundation of God's love and grace, then we can survive the storms of life. It's not always easy, but it's definitely worth the trouble—not only for our sake, but also for the sake of our children. After all, they're watching and waiting to follow our example.

QUESTIONS TO PONDER

1. Review the four key characteristics of effective limits and boundaries. Do the limits and boundaries you've set for your children meet these requirements? Why or why not? Do any changes need to be made?

2. Are the limits and boundaries you've set for your children grounded in your family's value system? If so, have you made your children aware of these connections? If not, what changes need to be made?

3. Is there a written list (or lists) of limits and boundaries posted somewhere in your home? Did your children help to compile the list(s)?

4. Are there parents who share your values with whom you can discuss appropriate limits and boundaries and other parenting issues? Why not set up a schedule of regular meetings or chat sessions?

5. Do you teach your children the importance of respecting limits and boundaries by your own example? How?

6. List all the responsibilities that must be met in your home and review them with your children. Which family member has the most to do? Do any changes need to be made in order for these responsibilities to be more equitably distributed?

6

DISCIPLINING WITH CONSEQUENCES, NOT PUNISHMENT

Scripture Link

Don't make your children angry by the way you treat them. Rather, bring them up with the discipline and instruction approved by the Lord.
                    —Ephesians 6:4 NLT

If you love your children, you will be prompt to discipline them.   —Proverbs 13:24b NLT

A wise child accepts a parent's discipline.
                    —Proverbs 13:1a NLT

obert Frost wrote a wonderful poem called "The Road Less Traveled." In this poem he talks about walking in the woods and coming to a place where the paths diverged—the proverbial fork in the road. He decided to take the road less traveled by, "and that has made all the difference."

When we come to a fork in the road, we have a decision to make: Which road should I take? For our children, this fork in the road, this "Y," represents an important decision: Whose value system will they choose to follow? The left side of the "Y" represents your family's values. At the end of this road is your family's North Star. The right side of the "Y" represents society's values—society's wants and desires and negative peer pressure. At the end of this road is the artificial star. The process of identifying your family's North Star, writing a family mission statement, empowering your children, and setting effective limits and boundaries will help your children to choose the right road—the road that God wants them to follow. But that's not enough to keep them on that road.

Children Need Consequences

As we discussed in the previous chapter, a child's natural tendency is to test the limits. All children get off track from time to time. That is to be expected. Yet, in most cases, consequences will get them back on track. When a child decides to change paths and walk toward the artificial star, there must be a consequence waiting for the child. Why a *consequence* and not a *punishment?* The answer lies in understanding the difference between the two.

Simply put, a consequence is a choice. For example, if a child chooses not to do his chores, then he has made the choice to receive a consequence such as losing a privilege or doing an additional chore. The choice is his, and the consequence becomes educational to the child. Consequences help teach children how to make wise choices, how to accept responsibility for their actions, and how to be held accountable for their choices. Consequences teach children that if they stay on point by following the family value system, obeying the house rules, and fulfilling responsibilities such as chores, positive things will happen—such as receiving verbal praise or a privilege of some kind. Likewise, they learn that if they get off point by rejecting the family values, disobeying the rules, or neglecting responsibilities such as chores, consequences will follow—such as losing a privilege or being assigned an additional chore.

Punishment, on the other hand, is punitive in nature, as the word itself infers. This is why, as I have observed, you'll never hear an expert in children's behavior use the word *punishment.* Unlike consequences, punishment does not guide the child back on point; in fact, often it guides the child farther off point! For a child to stay on the right path, she must feel loved. If she starts to associate punishment with the family star, she is likely to feel unloved and choose to follow the artificial star instead. Though punishment may cause a child to comply out of fear, its effect is always temporary. Punishment brings about short-term behavior change, whereas consequences bring about long-term behavior change.

When it comes to corporal punishment, it's hard to deny its short-term effectiveness—particularly with young children. Though some child development authorities condone corporal punishment as a method of disciplining children until a certain age (the recommended age limit varies, though many agree that paddling a child after age three can cause emotional scars), others say there is reason to question its long-term effectiveness. In their book *How to Talk So Kids Will Listen & Listen So Kids Will Talk,* Adele Faber and Elaine Mazlish ask parents to consider what children actually learn when their hands are slapped. Children learn, they suggest, that the only reason not to do something is to avoid having their hands slapped. As I see it, hand slapping doesn't give children the opportunity to learn that the real reason they are to follow family rules and behave properly is because this behavior is the right thing to do—in other words, because it keeps them on the path that God wants them to follow.

Though I didn't spank Curt and Beth when they were young, occasionally I would give them a slap on their hands when they touched something that I had asked them not to touch. Eventually, however, I discontinued that practice because it always made me feel empty inside. I decided, instead, to follow Carol's lead and send them to their room or take away a privilege. I have come to believe that consequences can effectively replace the rod in *every* situation. In addition to my own parenting experiences, I have several years worth of feedback from parents who tell me that effective consequences really do work. Unlike punishment, which is punitive in nature, consequences cause children much less reason to ever question or doubt if they are still loved. Personally, I believe that sparing the rod does not spoil the child *if effective consequences are used in its place.* In fact, I can say with confidence that parents who will be persistent and consistent in developing effective consequences will see positive long-term behavior change in their children.

Choosing Effective Consequences

Though some parents allow their children to "do as they please," most parents recognize the need for consequences when responding to their children's negative behavior. Interestingly enough, however, often parents repeat my courses because they still are unsuccessful in changing their children's negative behavior. Why? The key is learning to choose *effective* consequences. In addition to following a few guidelines, choosing effective consequences simply requires time and practice. Though there may be a "learning curve" involved in choosing consequences that work equally well for different children, there are some universal guidelines that will help to keep you on the right track.

As with limits and boundaries, consequences are effective only when they are clearly stated, reasonable, communicated in advance, and age-appropriate. The guidelines for setting effective limits and boundaries, presented in the previous chapter, can be applied to consequences as well. (See pp. 81-86 to review.) I recommend you review your list(s) of limits and boundaries and determine effective consequences for each prior to discussing these consequences with your children. Then, once you are in agreement, review the consequences with your children, adding them to the written list(s) of limits and boundaries you have already compiled. Remember that each child should have a separate list of limits and consequences, which may be posted in the kitchen or other high traffic area.

In addition to these basic guidelines, many experts recommend that effective consequences must be applied immediately after the violation has occurred, applied on a consistent basis, linked to the specific limit whenever possible (natural consequences), and increased if negative behavior continues (doubling up). We'll discuss natural consequences and doubling up in the remaining sections of this chapter. But first, let's take a moment to consider the importance of immediacy and consistency.

Obviously, children have a better chance of retaining the link between the limit and the consequence if the consequence is applied immediately after the limit has been exceeded. Likewise, a consequence has a much better chance of being effective if it is applied on a consistent basis. This is another reason it is so important for parents to discuss limits and consequences in advance.

Children naturally seek out the parent they know will offer the more favorable consequence! What's more, if parents give their children mixed messages, then the educational impact of any consequence is significantly minimized. To be effective, then, consequences must be both immediately and consistently applied.

PARENT POINT
Guidelines for Choosing Effective Consequences

Effective consequences are—
1. clear and reasonable
2. tied to expectations that have been communicated in advance
3. age-appropriate
4. applied immediately after the violation has occurred
5. applied on a consistent basis
6. linked to the specific limit whenever possible (natural consequences)
7. increased if negative behavior continues (doubling up)
8. presented as options, giving the child a choice

Natural Consequences

As we've seen, all consequences are educational because they offer a choice and a learning experience. Natural consequences, however, are particularly valuable. A natural consequence is a consequence that is linked to a specific limit. Let's consider a couple of examples using two universal struggles known to all parents.

The first universal struggle is mealtime. Whether we like it or not, the truth is that we cannot make our children eat. We can merely give them the *opportunity* to eat. And what is the natural consequence of choosing not to eat? That's right: hunger! I recommend you announce what time a meal will be served and what time it will be concluded (for example, 6:00–6:30 P.M.). Tell your children how much you would enjoy having them eat with you. However, if they choose not to come—or to come and not to eat—

that's their decision. (Obviously, younger children who cannot tell time need to be told when it's dinnertime.) The only comment you should make is that no other food will be served until the next meal. And if breakfast is the next meal, it's going to be a long wait!

Eventually, Joey tests this new limit. He arrives at 6:35 P.M. for dinner. He was playing outside and lost track of the time. Joey's parents walk him over to the list of rules and consequences posted on the refrigerator and calmly read the consequence to him. If he whines or yells, they tell him to take his behavior away from them or he will be given another consequence. The next morning, Joey's parents treat him to a very special breakfast and make no comments about the previous evening.

Why should they do that? Because they love him. After all, as Cline and Fay remind us in *Parenting with Love and Logic*, we're running a home, not a prison. God's love needs to occupy our home even when our children act badly. If Joey were to miss another dinner soon thereafter, however—either the following night or within a couple of days—then his parents should consider *not* having a special breakfast for him the following morning.

Although I am not a nutritionist, I do appreciate the need for children to eat portions from all the major food groups. I was raised in a home where we were not allowed to leave the table until we had eaten at least some of our vegetables. Unfortunately for me, the only cooked vegetable I liked was corn. I particularly disliked green beans, peas, spinach, broccoli, beets, and asparagus. Sometimes I tried to hide my vegetables in my potato skins or spill them onto the floor for my dog, Snoopy, to eat! Finally, when I went to college, I didn't have to eat those dreaded vegetables anymore. It wasn't until I married Carol that I learned to enjoy eating vegetables. She made green beans that didn't taste like green beans, and she put cheese on the broccoli and hollandaise sauce on the asparagus! The only vegetable I still won't eat under any circumstances is brussel sprouts. (If you happen to know how to make brussel sprouts taste like something other than brussel sprouts, please send me your recipe!)

You may be asking yourself why I'm telling you all this. The reason is that I agree with those experts who advise us not to make children eat food that doesn't taste good to them. If you *force* your children to eat food they don't like ("You're not leaving the table until you eat all of your vegetables!"), they will view it as punishment. Let's face it: Most children don't like eating certain foods or experimenting with new foods. So, as a concerned parent, what are you to do? I recommend you offer your children the opportunity to eat balanced meals each day, do your best to see that they are consuming *something* from each of the major food groups, and require them to take a children's vitamin every day. I also like this strategy suggested by Cline and Fay. When you are introducing a new food—or, I would add, a previously rejected food prepared in a different way—don't allow the children to try it! Tell them that this is *adult* food, and feed them hot dogs instead. While you're eating, go overboard in your demonstration of how much you like the new food. The next night, have the special food again, and once again, give the kids "children's food." Cline predicts that by the end of this second dinner, one of the children will demand to be allowed to try the new food. When this happens, tell the child that adults always behave in a mature manner when eating adult food and never spit it out. You get the idea! (See *Parenting with Love and Logic,* pp. 148-49.)

A second universal struggle is bedtime. Again, I concur with the experts who say that we can't make our children sleep; we can only give them the *opportunity* to sleep. Ultimately, our children make the choice of when they will sleep. So, what are we to do?

Let me share an example based on the approach Cline and Fay describe in their book. Let's say that Joey's bedtime is 8:00 P.M. That means that Joey must be ready for bed by 8:00 P.M. After kissing him goodnight, his parents tell him that he can stay awake as long as he wants, but that he must be quiet. No radio or television is allowed. However, he can play in his room. Joey loves this new freedom and plays in his room until late into the evening when he finally falls to sleep. His parents wake him up on time. (They are reasonably sure he didn't set the alarm clock last night.) Joey tells them that he is very tired and doesn't feel good. "Mom, I need to stay home today," he says. She calmly replies that he made the choice not to get enough sleep, and he is going to school today. Joey will have a very long day at school! Later that day, his parents act as if nothing happened the night before, avoiding their strong desire to say, "I told you so!" If Joey's parents are consistent, eventually Joey will learn from the natural consequence of being tired that the right choice is to get plenty of sleep.

You might want to take a slightly different approach to bedtime, however, if you have young children. Let's say that four-year-old Sissy is playing with her toys and it's time for bed. Her mother pleads, "Please, Sissy, it's time to come to bed." Each time Sissy screams in a louder pitch. Eventually, Mom says, "Fine. You can stay up a little longer tonight, but *tomorrow* you are going to bed on time." Obviously, Sissy learns that when she throws a temper tantrum, she gets her way. Some time later, after Mom has learned how to enforce effective consequences, she calmly tells Sissy that getting a good night's sleep is not only important to her health, but it's also an important family value. Then she tells Sissy that it's fifteen minutes until bedtime, and if she doesn't come right now there won't be time for a story. Sissy loves bedtime stories, and Mom knows that. Sissy may choose to continue watching television for fifteen minutes or to go upstairs and prepare for bed. If Sissy really loves those bedtime stories, she will go upstairs and get ready for bed.

What if Sissy decided, instead, to pass on the bedtime story because she was playing with her favorite toy? What should Mom do then? First of all, Mom should remind Sissy that she has to be in bed by 8:00 P.M., and it's now 7:45 P.M. If Sissy chooses to play for those fifteen minutes, that's her choice; but she still has to be in bed with lights out by 8:00 P.M. If she isn't, then she loses a privilege to be determined by her parents. Privileges are very important to young children and can be very effective when used as consequences. Remember, we are not making the choice for Sissy, but we are making it easier for her to make the right choice.

"Doubling Up"

As I mentioned previously, what I call "doubling up" is a way of increasing the stakes of a particular consequence in order to motivate behavior change. "Doubling up" works with both natural and contrived consequences.

I like to use the example of curfew to illustrate the concept of "doubling up." Let's say that Joey's parents give him an 8:00 P.M.

curfew with a thirty-minute reduction as the consequence for violating the curfew. Joey has never seen his parents enforce house rules before, so he decides to come home at 8:15. His parents walk over to the list of limits and consequences posted in the kitchen and change the curfew, showing Joey that his new curfew is 7:30 P.M. Joey decides that his parents are serious about the 8:00 curfew, so he comes home the next night at 7:55—five minutes early, he thinks. After reminding him that his curfew had been changed to 7:30, they tell him that the consequence now will be doubled because he missed curfew again. So, what is Joey's new curfew? The answer is 6:30 P.M. The first time Joey missed curfew, his parents moved his curfew back thirty minutes. The second time he missed curfew, they "doubled up" the thirty minutes to one hour. If Joey doesn't "wake up" and start coming home on time, his next curfew will be 4:30 (one hour "doubles up" to two hours)!

When I first began suggesting this approach, parents would tell me that the concept of "doubling up" when a child continued to violate curfew worked very well. Their only frustration was not being sure how soon to return to the original curfew after the child had corrected his or her behavior. Based on my readings on the subject, I have come to believe there is only one valid recommendation: Parents should remain in the position of control by moving the curfew back up very slowly and painfully. Returning to the original curfew right away—before the lesson has "stuck," so to speak—can result in setbacks. Setbacks can cause what I call yo-yo parenting, and no one wants to become a yo-yo!

Here are some other examples of "doubling up" on a consequence: from one night of being grounded to two nights, or one weekend to two weekends; from taking the garbage out once a week to twice a week. As you strive to "hold out" despite much grumbling and pleading and even signs of changed behavior, keep reminding yourself of two things: First, you're after long-term behavior change, and second, children who learn to respect limits also learn to respect the law. If we want consequences to be effective, then we must be willing to increase those consequences until the child's behavior is back "on point."

When Natural Consequences Don't Work

During my first year of teaching parenting courses, an irate mother told me that the concept of consequences was ineffective with her sixteen-year-old son. She had given her son the chore of unloading the dishwasher; and when he had failed to do so, she had told him that his consequence was to empty it out *two* times in a row. When this announcement had failed to bring about change, she had told him that he had to unload the dishwasher four consecutive times. Again, he didn't obey. Because the consequence relied upon his compliance, he was able to avoid the consequence altogether. Sometimes tying the consequence to the particular limit or house rule is not the best idea.

I suggested to this mother that she might try a new idea of mine called "the brown bag." First, she was to write her son's name on a brown lunch bag. Then she was to write four privileges on small pieces of paper and put them in the brown bag. One of these privileges, I explained, should be something very important to her son. We decided to call this most important privilege "the big kahuna." For her sixteen-year-old son, the "big kahuna" was driving her car. Finally, she was to tell her son that if he did not unload the dishwasher, he would have to put his hand in the bag and pull out a piece of paper. His consequence would be to lose whatever privilege was written on the paper. He would have a 25 percent chance of losing the privilege of driving the car just because he didn't want to spend five minutes unloading the dishwasher. It would be his choice.

When the mom came to the next parenting class, she had a huge smile on her face! Her sixteen-year-old son had started to do his chore because he had realized that driving his mother's car was an important privilege he didn't want to lose. It worked because his mother had identified an effective "big kahuna," yet she had kept it reasonable. She had decided that for her son, losing the privilege of driving her car for one weekend was reasonable. Other parents might have chosen to make the restriction two weekends or one full week, depending upon a particular child's past behavior pattern.

I'm pleased to say that "the brown bag" has been working well for parents ever since. It works equally with children of all ages whenever a natural or "linked" consequence isn't effective or appropriate. I encourage you to give it a try!

PARENT POINT
Using "The Brown Bag"

1. Write your child's name on the outside of a brown lunch sack.
2. Identify four privileges that your child enjoys; one of these should be something very important to your child—the "big kahuna." Remember, however, to keep it reasonable. (Some parents find that their children are more agreeable to the idea if they are allowed to participate in choosing the privileges that go into the bag. When it comes to the "big kahuna," however, parents should have the final say.) Remember, also, that your child's "big kahuna" can change, and you may need to make a substitution.
3. Write each privilege on a small piece of paper and put it into the bag.
4. Whenever a natural consequence isn't appropriate, have your child draw a paper from the bag to determine what privilege he or she will lose. Then put the paper back into the bag for next time.
5. On the child's list of limits and consequences, be sure to put "the brown bag" under the consequences column.

Avoiding Unreasonable Consequences

We've already considered why a consequence must be reasonable in order to be effective. Yet just when does a consequence—whether natural or otherwise—become unreasonable and punitive in nature? How do you know? This is a troubling question for many parents. Let me share a story from my youth to help answer this question.

By spring of my senior year in high school, I was madly in love. We'll call her Sue. It was time for the big event of the year: senior prom. Sue and I were going with my best friend, Howdy, and his date. He arranged for us to borrow his neighbor's baby blue T-Bird convertible. Howdy and I rented baby blue tuxedos to match. We were going to be the coolest dudes at the prom, and I was going to be with the prettiest girl in school. Sue's parents were reactive in nature; and because their daughter was a strong-willed child, there was always a lot of conflict in the family. One week before the prom, Sue got in trouble, and her parents refused to let her go to the prom. I was devastated by her parent's action. I felt as if I had done something bad. I always felt after their decision that Sue's parents were wanting to punish me as much as their daughter. My senior year ended on a very low note.

If you want to avoid giving unreasonable consequences, I suggest you follow two rules of thumb. First, a consequence is unreasonable when it impacts other people. For example, never keep your child from playing in a ball game—or participating in a play or other performance—because that will be detrimental to the other members of the team or group. Likewise, if one child is misbehaving, don't allow that child's consequence to punish other members of the family. So, if Joey has been bad, don't cancel the family picnic. Instead, choose a consequence that will affect Joey only—and, of course, that will be effective in bringing about long-term behavior change. (See pp. 95-99 to review the guidelines for choosing effective consequences.)

Second, never set a consequence when you are angry. Generally speaking, we are incapable of thinking clearly when we are angry. I know this to be true from my own parenting experiences. Often I would give Curt or Beth a consequence that was unreasonable—or even punitive in nature—when I was angry. So, if you are angry, tell your child that you will set a consequence the following day, after you have had a chance to calm down, pray, and think clearly. If possible, it's wise for both parents to determine the consequence together to ensure that objectivity is maintained.

An important goal of this book is to help you become a *proactive* parent. The proactive approach, then, is to develop limits and consequences for those limits simultaneously and in advance, which will help to ensure long-term behavior change. There will be times, however, when your child exhibits an unanticipated behavior for which you haven't thought of a consequence. Unless this behavior involves your child's safety, which would necessitate an immediate response, I recommend you give your child a warning the first time. Then give yourself adequate time to identify both a limit and a consequence that address this behavior. After you have reviewed both the limit and the consequence with your child, add them to his or list of limits and consequences. By using this method, you will avoid giving an unreasonable consequence when angry while simultaneously creating a system that properly corrects bad behavior.

If your children are to respect the limits and boundaries you set for them, you must be willing to enforce consequences when those limits and boundaries are violated. Always remember, however, that these consequences must be *reasonable* and *effective* if they are to bring about long-term behavior change.

QUESTIONS TO PONDER

1. What are the characteristics of *effective* consequences? How do effective consequences help your children to stay on the path that God wants them to follow?

2. Why is punishment an ineffective disciplinary tool?

3. What unreasonable consequences have you given your children in the past? What can you do to avoid giving unreasonable consequences in the future?

4. Have you determined an effective consequence for each of the limits that you have set for your children? Have you compiled a list of limits and consequences for each of your children and reviewed these lists with each of them?

5. Have you identified the "big kahuna" for each of your children? What other privileges might you add to a "brown bag" for each child? (Remember, you may find it beneficial to involve your child in this process—though you should have the last word on the "big kahuna.")

7

TEACHING YOUR CHILDREN
DELAYED GRATIFICATION

Scripture Link

Keep away from [sinful] desires because they fight against your very souls. Be careful how you live among your unbelieving neighbors. Even if they accuse you of doing wrong, they will see your honorable behavior, and they will believe and give honor to God.
—1 Peter 2:11b-12 NLT

I consider that our present sufferings are not worth comparing with the glory that will be revealed in us. . . . But if we hope for what we do not yet have, we wait for it patiently. In the same way, the Spirit helps us in our weakness.   *—Romans 8:18, 25-26a NIV*

We also pray that you will be strengthened with his glorious power so that you will have all the patience and endurance you need.   *—Colossians 1:11a NLT*

The Search Institute, which was founded in 1958 by Merton T. Strommen to study the attitudes and needs of youth, has identified forty common threads or "developmental assets" evident among youth who thrive. The book *What Kids Need to Succeed: Proven, Practical Ways to Raise Good Kids* (1997, Peter Benson, Judy Galbraith, Pamela Espeland) documents these assets and describes what parents, schools, communities, and the church can do to help youth acquire them. According to survey findings, children who acquire thirty or more assets demonstrate a much

105

higher percentage of positive or desired behaviors. I'd like to focus on one desired behavior that deserves the special attention of all parents: delayed gratification.

Why Is Delayed Gratification So Important?

Today we hear much more about *instant* gratification than we do about *delayed* gratification. Our society tells our children to live for today, to do what feels good today—in other words, to follow the alluring artificial star. In contrast, delayed gratification is a learned behavior that empowers our children to do what is right today, to say no to pleasures that could be destructive to themselves and/or others—in other words, to resist the temptations of the alluring artificial star. Delayed gratification, then, is crucial to our children's ability to stay "on point."

Simply put, delayed gratification is the ability to wait. You might say that we teach our children delayed gratification whenever and however we help them to acquire the developmental assets of restraint and responsibility. Children who learn to practice restraint learn to live within a reasonable set of limits and boundaries—as opposed to feeling they are entitled to do as they please. Children who learn to be responsible learn to be confident in their own abilities and decisions—as opposed to giving in to peer pressure and placing blame on others. Children who develop restraint and responsibility, then, are more capable and confident when it comes to saying "no" to behavior that is outside the family value system. In other words, as I mentioned in chapter 2, they are more likely to say "no" to temptations such as premarital sex, drugs, and other destructive behaviors. And when they do—when they learn to practice delayed gratification—they discover that self-control and self-respect go hand in hand.

Delayed Gratification Must Be a "Family Affair"

With the artificial star growing on a daily basis, it's vital that we parents model the family North Star on a daily basis. We cannot expect our children to be able to delay their desire for gratification unless we model this behavior ourselves. I learned this well from my own parents, who were my best teachers when it came to delayed gratification. Perhaps a glimpse into my past will help you to understand why I believe so strongly that delayed gratification must be a "family affair."

Although my dad and mom were blessed in many ways, one of their biggest blessings was that they were neither wealthy nor dirt poor. They both worked, and their combined income truly placed them in the middle class. My dad, therefore, had an "excuse" that helped him deal with the challenges associated with delayed gratification. If we kids wanted him to buy us something, he would simply say, "We can't afford it." Though our parents gave us money to go to the movies or to buy a coke at the local drugstore, we were "on our own" for the majority of things that were not considered personal or family needs. Consequently, we learned to do work in the neighborhood in order to earn our own money. I cut many lawns and shoveled many driveways in the winter. My best source of income, though, was babysitting. I was the only male in the neighborhood who babysat, so I was in constant demand. Thanks again to the guidance of Mom and Dad, some of our earnings went into the bank for college spending money. They told us that they would pay for our college tuition and room and board, but we would have to provide our own spending money. Though our grandfather occasionally gave us some money that went into the bank for college, we knew we would have to work hard and save—practice delayed gratification—in order to have enough. Each of us had his or her own bank account. I always loved seeing the entries in red ink, because that was the interest the bank was paying!

Presents came twice a year: birthday and Christmas. Unfortunately for me, my birthday is in December. I always felt cheated because I was convinced that some of my birthday presents were saved for Christmas. My parents denied my accusations, but I knew that was the truth. Of course, years later, I came to understand. I also came to appreciate the fact that our parents didn't give us whatever we wanted when we wanted it—again, delayed gratification. Instead, we learned to wait for those special occasions with great anticipation and much gratitude.

Before school began each year, our parents would buy us some clothes. Again, I felt I was "cheated," for I had an older brother. My mom would save his clothes, and I would get them three years later. Both my brother and my sister got more new clothes than I did, which I resented immensely at the time. Of course, once again I came to understand the practicality and wisdom in this budgeting necessity. I'll never forget my senior year, when madras was king. All "cool" shirts and shorts were madras. Some stores copied the style, but we kids new the difference. I had three imitation long-sleeve madras shirts. I wore one on Monday, one on Tuesday, and one on Wednesday. Then, Monday's shirt became Thursday's, and Tuesday's shirt became Friday's. It was a very simple system, and it worked well. I knew that if I wanted an authentic madras shirt, I would have to pay for it myself. So I decided that I could live without one just fine! All those lessons in delayed gratification had taken hold.

Throughout my childhood, I had friends whose families were poorer than mine, as well as friends whose families were wealthier than mine. Consequently, there were times when I felt blessed and times when I felt a little deprived, particularly during my freshman year of high school when I attended a large school fed by several adjacent communities. Even so, the consistent example and guidance of my parents helped me realize the importance of practicing delayed gratification—a practice I carried with me into adulthood.

I really began to appreciate all those lessons I'd learned in delayed gratification after I got married. Thankfully, I married a woman who had learned delayed gratification from her family as well. Our apartment was furnished entirely by donations from family and friends, but we didn't care! By saving as much as we could each month, we were able to put a down payment on a townhouse in just a few short years. Then, within one year, we were able to double our investment as the resale value of the townhouse soared. That initial down payment grew nicely over the years as we bought and sold several houses. By continuing to save through the years and practice wise money management—thanks, again, to all those lessons we learned from our parents—we were able to build savings for emergencies, future purchases, college educations for the children, and our own retirement. As we did those things, we were able to pass the lessons we'd learned on to our own children, including the valuable lesson of delayed gratification.

One of the most important lessons in delayed gratification that Carol and I passed on to Curt and Beth was simply this: We didn't give them everything they wanted! When we don't give our children everything they want, they learn how to earn money, how to save money, and how to spend money appropriately. Again, modeling those behaviors ourselves is crucial. Earning and saving money are lessons that come more easily to all of us—parents and children alike. It's learning how to spend money appropriately that usually gives us trouble! Let me suggest four simple practices that can help you and your family to stay on track.

1. Create a family budget.

If you are going to "walk the talk" of delayed gratification, then you must begin by creating a family budget. A budget is simply a declaration of your sources of income and the various monthly expenses that will deplete that income. Creating a family budget and adjusting it monthly according to your projected income and expenses enables you to live within your means and avoid accumulating debt. Your projected expenses include both fixed expenses (e.g., mortgage or rent, food, insurance, transportation, taxes, church and other charitable giving, and savings) and variable expenses (e.g., clothes, entertainment, and eating out). Your values will determine which items are permanently fixed in your budget and which items vary based upon the amount of money left after meeting all fixed expenses.

Unfortunately, many families today allow society's values, rather than their family values, to create their budgets. As a result, savings has become a variable expense, rather than a fixed expense, in many family budgets. Likewise, eating out, which should always be a variable expense, has become a fixed expense in the budgets of many busy families. So, as you create your budget, I recommend you keep your family mission statement close at hand to remind yourself of the values your family considers important. After all, it is your true values—not society's values or your "wants"—that should determine the fixed and variable expenses of your family budget. Once you have agreed on the fixed items in your budget, which should always include contributions to savings and to church and other charitable organizations, then you can negotiate the variable items without compromising your family values.

Because our children mirror us, it is important for us to help them become knowledgeable about the budgeting process. As you review the budget together, take this opportunity to reinforce your values by explaining why savings is such an important category, and why making regular contributions to your church and other charitable organizations is more important than always eating out for dinner or always having a new car. Involving your children in budget discussions helps them to understand that sometimes sacrifices need to be made for the good of the family. If you want to take a family vacation, for example, tell the children how much it will cost and explain what items need to be sacrificed in order to save the necessary amount. Learning how to live within a budget is not only an important lesson in and of itself; it also is an effective way to teach the value of delayed gratification.

There are many excellent resources and financial "experts" available to assist your family in the area of budgeting. One such expert who does a wonderful job helping families learn how to retire their debt and become good stewards of their financial resources is Dave Ramsey, author of *Financial Peace* and host of the nationally syndicated *Dave Ramsey* talk radio show. Ramsey is one of several experts who recommend using an envelope system in which cash is deposited into various envelopes designated for specific categories in the family budget. The idea is that once the cash in a particular envelope is gone, no more money may be spent on that category. Families who use the envelope system tell me that it helps them stick to the budget and avoid overspending. They say that it's a good way to break dangerous habits such as whipping out a credit card for impulse buys or making a quick trip to the nearest ATM whenever cash is running low. One of the biggest problems we have in our country today is the billions of dollars of credit card debt. Every time we place that plastic card down on the counter, we are telling our children that we don't practice delayed gratification. I encourage you to consult the work of Ramsey and other financial experts for more information about this and other ideas for keeping your family debt free.

There's no question that money is one of the most divisive issues in families today, generating much tension, stress, anxiety, conflict, anger, and rage. This is why I agree with Dave Ramsey when he says that we have a *moral* responsibility to put our financial houses in order. For me, this includes teaching our children how to live on a budget. Successful budgeting is not only an effective antidote to family conflict; it's also one of the most valuable lessons in delayed gratification we can ever provide for our children.

2. Give your children regular allowances.

Allowances are an item that should be included in every family budget. I agree with those financial experts who explain that the purpose of an allowance is to teach children to respect money and recognize its value. I also agree with those experts who say that allowances should not be tied to household chores or a child's behavior. As I noted in chapter 5, helping around the house and behaving according to house rules should be expectations of *all* family members. When allowances are used as a reward or a consequence, children don't learn that behaving properly and doing chores are responsibilities of every family member.

Because allowances are intended to teach children to be responsible with money, they should be given with certain requirements. First, children should be required to use a portion of their allowance toward certain "fixed expenses" of their own, which are dictated by your family values. I support the belief of many experts and parents, for example, that a child should regularly give a fixed percentage of his or her allowance to the church. When children fill out a church commitment card and make regular payments to the church themselves, they feel part of the giving process and they learn how to be a responsible member of the church. Too often parents give their children money for church, which teaches them very little if anything about the spirit and nature of true giving. Second, a child should be required to put aside a fixed percentage of his or her allowance for college or other goals that will require future savings.

Beyond these two requirements, a child should be allowed to make decisions about how to spend or save the remaining money—as long as family values are not compromised by their decisions. We know that children learn delayed gratification when they save money to buy something later. However, another important life skill is learned when they impulsively blow all their allowance at once and have to wait for their next allowance to buy something that they really want. This valuable lesson also helps to keep children from becoming impulsive buyers as adults.

3. Practice "reasonable and customary expenses."

One of the most helpful concepts related to delayed gratification that I share with parents came to me after a couple of frustrating experiences with my son, Curt. The first was when Curt introduced me to Tommy—Hilfiger, that is. He told me that he needed a Tommy shirt, and I instantly thought of the old song "Tommy" by The Who. Talk about a generation gap! "Okay," I said, "where do we buy a Tommy shirt?" He said, "At the mall." I knew that, once again, Curt was the new kid on the block and, once again, was struggling to fit in. So, off we went.

I have a vivid memory of riding up the escalator at the mall and, as we reached the top, seeing the false god Tommy. He was glorious. He was handsome. He was stylish. At first glance, I liked Tommy. The styles and colors of clothes were fantastic. Then Curt proceeded to show me the shirt that he just had to have. "Here it is, Dad," he said. "Isn't it great? Everyone has one." Now, those years of shoveling snow and cutting grass and babysitting had made a permanent impression on me, so I quickly put on my "sunglasses" and tried to see Tommy for what he really was. When I looked at the price tag, I almost fainted. "I am not paying this amount of money for a shirt. My shirts don't cost half this much. No way, Jose!" I exclaimed. We had a very quiet ride home.

I was both angry and guilty. I was angry that some clothes for young kids cost so much, and I was angry that some parents were buying their children these clothes; I also felt guilty for not buying what I knew would make Curt happy. I wanted to help him fit in with the kids at school, but I knew we couldn't pay that much for a shirt. Later that year after Carol went back to work, we were able to buy a few Tommy shirts for Curt. It's funny, though. When I finally gave him the Tommy shirt, I experienced a moment of *delayed satisfaction*. I had expected lots of hugs and praises but got very few. As Bill Oliver, creator of the parenting program *Parent to Parent*, says, parenting is the art of dissatisfaction!

The next hurdle involved a false god named Michael—Jordan, that is. This was the god of expensive tennis shoes, and he was called "Air Jordan" because he could fly through the air! Because Curt was such a highly ranked tennis player and was sponsored by the Wilson sporting goods company, he could buy all of his equipment, including tennis shoes, directly from them. All of Curt's friends had Air Jordan tennis shoes, and he wanted them as well. Wilson, however, didn't carry Air Jordan tennis shoes. There we were in the same predicament again.

Finally, the old lightbulb turned on and I came up with a solution—one that has helped numerous families deal with the Tommys and Michaels of the world. The idea came to me as I recalled my days as an auditor. In those days, one of my responsibilities was to audit expense accounts. I knew that the company was allowed by the Internal Revenue Service to deduct only "reasonable and customary" charges. That's why there was a company policy stating that when employees traveled on business, we were not allowed to stay at the most expensive hotels—though we didn't have to stay in a "roach motel," either. Instead, we were expected to stay in hotels with reasonable accommodations. Likewise, we were not to eat at the most expensive restaurants—though we didn't have to eat at McDonalds every night, either. You get the idea. As I thought more about it, I began to wonder, *Why don't I use this concept with my children?* I couldn't think of any reason why it wouldn't work.

So, I told Curt that I would give him $50.00 for his next pair of tennis shoes—the price he would pay for a pair of good tennis shoes from the Wilson company—and he would have to pay the difference. He wasn't thrilled with the idea, but he really wanted those Air Jordans; so, he agreed to pay the difference. As it turned out, he quickly discovered that those particular shoes do not function well on the tennis court. He wore out the toes very quickly. Curt learned several lessons with his purchase. First, he learned that keeping up with his peers can be a costly adventure. Second, he learned that sometimes our wants do not satisfy our needs.

The "reasonable and customary expenses" concept is helping more and more parents to deal with the Tommys and Michaels of the world. They say that it gives their children a better appreciation of money and helps them learn to deal with financial peer pressure. However, as with any delayed gratification concept, it doesn't work unless parents model it first by being reasonable purchasers themselves. If parents buy their clothing and other household items at reasonable prices, then their children will understand why they should do the same.

PARENT POINT
Putting "Reasonable and Customary Expenses" into Practice

1. To determine a "reasonable and customary" amount for any given purchase, price the item at several reasonably priced stores or vendors.

2. Average the prices to determine a reasonable and customary amount.

3. For items that are included in the family budget (e.g., clothes, shoes, school supplies, etc.), agree to pay the reasonable and customary amount and give your child the option of paying the difference from his or her own money.

4. For items that may fall outside the family budget (e.g., personal wants/desires, activities/entertainment above budgeted amounts or allowances, and so forth), allow your child to save money for the full purchase.

---

4. Allow your children to earn extra money.

Children who learn to practice delayed gratification also learn to save money. Actually, the two go hand-in-hand. In addition to learning to save a portion of their allowance for future purchases, most children soon become interested in finding ways to earn extra money. Because the issue of earning extra money takes on new dimensions as children become old enough to be employed outside the home, this is a matter that needs to be addressed as a family.

Many older children want to work after school and on weekends as a means of earning extra money. Experts who study children's development claim that a part-time job is fine during the school year as long as the job doesn't exceed sixteen to twenty hours a week. Regrettably, some children work six to eight hours *a day*—after school and on weekends—just so that they can buy a car. Contrary to popular belief, a car is not a necessity for a teenager; and it should not take precedence over important family values. If you believe involvement in the church is important to your children, then they need to have time to attend church and participate in the youth program and other activities. If you want your children to go to college, then they need to have enough time to study and do their homework. If you believe extracurricular activities such as sports, art, and music are important to your children's development, then they need time for these activities. And if you believe it's important to spend time together as a family, then you need to have some time available each week for doing just that. There's nothing wrong with allowing your child to take a part-time job as long as that job doesn't get in the way of your family's values. (By the way, we must set the example for our children by not allowing our own jobs to interfere with family values. I'll say more about this later in the book.) If and when it does, then it's time to reevaluate the reason for the job and discuss other ways your child might earn extra money.

In addition to jobs outside the home, our children can earn extra income by doing jobs in or around the home. I will always remember spending an entire summer painting the large cyclone fence in our backyard. My parents paid me as a contractor. It was a win/win proposition because my parents saved money, I was at home every day, and I made good money.

As with allowances, children should be required to give a fixed percentage of their earnings to the church and a fixed percentage to savings. Again, this practice not only teaches them wise money management but also responsibility and resistance. And, after all, that's what delayed gratification is all about!

Please, please, please, model delayed gratification for your children. Remember that children who "catch" delayed gratification— who learn to save money to buy something later—are more

willing and able to say "no" to destructive pleasures such as premarital sex and drugs as they get older.

QUESTIONS TO PONDER

1. In what ways do you model delayed gratification for your children?

2. How do counter the artificial star's support for instant gratification in your home?

3. Have you considered which retail companies are "reasonable and customary" for your family? Have you discussed this with your children?

4. Have you discussed the regular contribution amount that each child will be making to the church?

5. Have you established a savings account for each child?

6. What opportunities does each child have for earning extra money? Have you determined the total number of hours each child is allowed to work outside the home without compromising your family values?

CREATING A LOVING HOME

*So now I am giving you a new commandment:
Love each other. Just as I have loved you,
you should love each other. Your love
for one another will prove to the world
that you are my disciples.*

—*John 13:34 NLT*

8

IMPROVING COMMUNICATION SKILLS IN YOUR HOME

("You Can't Hear Me; I Can't Hear You")

Scripture Link

Listen, for I have worthy things to say.
—Proverbs 8:6 NIV

So encourage each other and build each other up.
—1 Thessalonians 5:11 NLT

I'll meet you halfway." That was always my position on communicating with my children. I felt pretty good about that position, too, because it was far better than the position my father took with me. With my dad, it was always up to me to initiate a conversation. I can't think of a single time when my dad came into my room to talk to me. My dad was raised in a home where the sharing of feelings and the exchange of ideas was not a commonplace event. So, when I was growing up, my siblings and I always went to our mom whenever we needed to talk. My mom created an environment in our home that supported effective communication. Her unconditional love for her children helped me and my brother and sister to easily find the courage to talk to her even when we were admitting a mistake. Actually, she instinctively came to us first most of the time.

So, I was determined to be a different kind of dad; I was going to "stay in the loop" with Curt and Beth. I was ignorant, however, about the time and effort required to have effective communication with my family, and we all suffered the consequences. If only I had known then what I know now. For example, I know now that we parents must be sensitive to body language—both our own and our children's. I know now that children under the age of ten communicate 80 percent of the time through body language rather than words. I know now that we aren't born good listeners; we must train our brains to listen. I know now that we often inhibit conversation with our children either by being angry or by being unavailable. I know now that we need to leave our work troubles at the doorstep before entering the home. I know now that there is a direct relationship between effective communication in the home and a loving and supportive home environment. I know now that there are many wonderful resources available to help us become effective communicators—especially better listeners.

This chapter is the culmination of all that I have learned in the area of communication. Its purpose is twofold: to help you improve the communication in your home, and to whet your appetite for even more information.

As I look back over my years of fatherhood, I realize that I made many mistakes. I didn't leave my work troubles at the doorstep. I didn't try to tailor my communication style to meet each child's needs, as I should have. I admit that, actually, there were many times when I failed to meet Curt or Beth halfway. I realize there were numerous times when I wore my "sunglasses" and failed to see the world through their eyes. (Our sunglasses, you'll remember, are the life experiences and attitudes that have colored the way we view things.) Consequently, my children mostly went to their mother for advice and support, leaving me out of the very loop that I wanted to be inside. As I look back, I recognize that every member of the family, including me, suffered from my inability to be an effective communicator. Curt's death was my wake-up call, and with God's help, I was able to change. If you read this chapter with an open mind, you, too, can make some constructive changes in your life—and, best of all, without having to receive any wake-up call of your own.

Avoid a "One Size Fits All" Approach

Whenever I teach parenting classes on effective communication, I emphasize the danger of a "one size fits all" approach. As we discussed in chapter 3, children come in all shapes, sizes, and personalities. And just as children have different personality traits, they also have different communication styles or preferences. In order to communicate more effectively, we must recognize these differences and adjust our style of communicating accordingly.

When it comes their assertiveness in communicating, most children tend to fall closer to one end of the spectrum than the other. Generally speaking, we can classify our children as being more assertive than nonassertive, or more nonassertive than assertive. Let's consider a few general guidelines for communicating with each.

1. Communicating with the nonassertive child.

First, be intentional about the *where*. On page 122, there are two figures connected by a horizontal line. The one on the right represents a parent, and the one on the left represents a nonassertive child. This child is shy and reluctant to share his feelings. Perhaps he was born shy, or perhaps he has had some bad experiences associated with sharing his feelings. Either way, he tends to keep his feelings deep inside. The vertical line that is drawn through the horizontal line represents the child's comfort zone. To communicate most effectively with your child, you must "meet" the shy child in his comfort zone. If you are only willing to meet him halfway ("If you have something you want to talk about, come find me"), then the child may never really open up and share his feelings.

My son, Curt, was a nonassertive child. I eventually learned that if I wanted to have a meaningful conservation with Curt in our house, I had to meet him in his comfort zone: normally, his room. In that respect, Curt was not the exception. Parents often tell me that their shy child spends a lot of time in his or her room—with the door closed. They do this because they feel safe and secure in their rooms. This is why experts agree that one of the best places to have a meaningful conversation with the nonassertive child—or

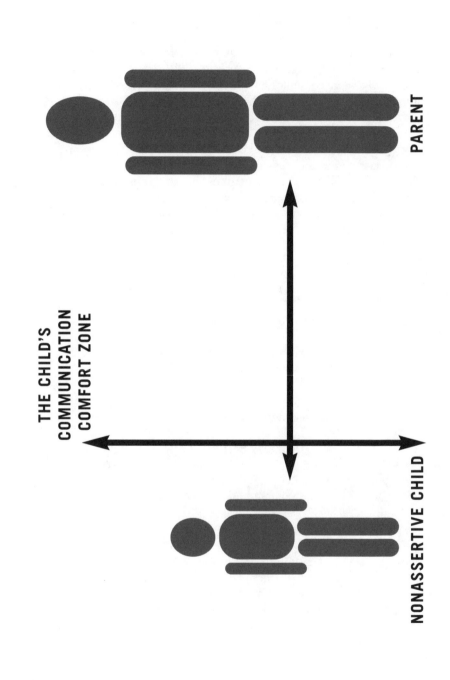

THE CHILD'S
COMMUNICATION
COMFORT ZONE

PARENT

NONASSERTIVE CHILD

any child, for that matter—is in the child's bedroom. Other shy children might consider a tree house or playhouse or fort to be a place of comfort and security. The particular place isn't important. The important thing is to identify your child's "comfort zone," the place where the child feels most comfortable, so that you may talk together without any barriers to hinder the flow of words or hide his or her true feelings.

Your child's comfort zone, then, is generally the best place to go if you have a serious issue to discuss or if you need to correct your child's behavior, voice your displeasure about a recent situation, or cover an issue that could be embarrassing to the child. Again, your child's bedroom is usually a good choice; however, all children are different, and you will find other places of comfort. By the way, as your child gets older, don't be surprised when he or she begins initiating conversations in *your* comfort zones! My son, Curt, would often ask me a difficult question at a sporting event, particularly if my team was winning the game!

Of course, your child's comfort zone is not the only place where you can communicate effectively with your nonassertive child. Regular communication about your child's everyday activities and interests is essential for a healthy parent-child relationship and a loving home environment, and this kind of communication can take place at the kitchen table, in the family room, in the car, and many other places.

Second, be intentional about the *when*. As I just acknowledged, regular communication about your child's everyday activities and interests is so important. When Curt was very young and I was constantly traveling away from home, he and I would go to McDonalds and have lunch together each Saturday—just the two of us. This was my chance to find out what he had done during the week and reconnect as a father and son. Unfortunately, as he got older and I quit traveling, I quit taking him to McDonalds because the need wasn't as apparent to me. That was a huge mistake on my part! Carol, on the other hand, was always really good at connecting with Curt and "drawing him out" on a regular basis. When he was younger, she would connect with him each day while reading to him, playing with him, and talking with him in the car. As he got older, she had more opportunities for these talks in the car while taking him to and from his many practices and lessons.

In addition to communicating with nonassertive children in these kinds of ways on a daily basis, we need to allow time each week for an extended one-on-one conversation. Remember, nonassertive children are generally not as prone to seek us out and initiate communication as more assertive children are.

Of course, there will be times, though less frequent, when your nonassertive child will seek you out. There were times when Carol and I would be talking in the kitchen, and Curt would come into the room and pull on my pant leg. "Daddy, I need to talk to you right now," he would say. Our natural reaction was to tell Curt to come back later. Our first response, then, was to say that he must learn to respect our space and not to interrupt. I later learned, however, that we parents are taking a big risk with this position. It's very likely that the nonassertive child won't come back. It's also very likely that if we keep telling him not to interrupt us, he'll quit coming to us at all. This is why I recommend you avoid having meaningful conversations with your spouse, or another adult, until after the children have gone to bed. Or, if you must discuss something that can't wait, explain that you need ten to fifteen minutes of uninterrupted time, go into your room, and close the door. Remember, you'll never know what your child might tell you unless you stop to listen. Perhaps your child wants to tell you that someone offered her a cigarette, or that some bully was picking on her on the bus. As early as the fourth grade, he may want to tell you that someone offered him a marijuana joint. Whenever your nonassertive child comes to you to talk, please treat this occasion as something special and give the child your full and undivided attention.

When you are the one initiating a more serious discussion, remember that it's never a good idea to surprise your nonassertive child, catching him or her "off guard." As parents regularly affirm, nonassertive children like to be prepared for these discussions. I recommend you give your child some advance warning that you'd like to talk later in the child's room—perhaps at bedtime. You might even bring some cookies with you in order to reinforce the love that you feel for the child. As I've learned through the years, children open up more easily when they know that you really care about them—which leads me to our next point.

Third, be intentional about the *how*. Even if we've been intentional about the *where and when,* we can still "blow it" with the *how!* So often we forget to take off our "sunglasses" before opening our mouths. The result is that we fail to see things through the eyes of the child and, therefore, communicate our love and care. I'll say more about this later in the chapter. For now, let's consider a common scenario. A mom wants to know why her daughter received a low grade on her report card. So she immediately begins with a list of questions. Did she turn her homework in late? Did she spend too much time watching television and not enough time studying? Did she have trouble understanding the teacher? These are the kinds of questions we ask when we're wearing our "sunglasses" instead of trying to see the world through our children's eyes. If a shy child believes we have already drawn a conclusion, she will go along with us and not try to present her point of view. Or she might feel that the questions have "backed her into a corner" and simply quit responding. I have learned that making "small" talk first is helpful with many shy children. However, for others, the strategy of talking around the subject can be a huge failure. Experiment to see which tactic works better with your own child.

Let's say that your son, Joey, got a D in math. Historically, Joey gets B's and occasionally C's. How should you discuss this? First, try to let Joey keep the ownership of the grade by asking him for his opinions and feelings before expressing your own. For example, you might say, "Joey, how do you feel about getting a D in math?" and "I need you to explain to me why you received this grade." After Joey has told you how he feels and explained why he received the grade, then share your feelings with Joey. Be careful to express *disappointment* rather than *anger*; anger often causes a shy child to "shut down" and quit talking. Problem-solve the situation together by identifying the actions that need to occur in order for Joey to get a better grade on his next report card. Once you've done this, don't just walk out of the room. Talk about something else—something that brings praise to Joey. You might say, "Joey, your other grades were very good," or "How is practice going this week?" or "How are your music lessons going?" Remember that your objective is to leave Joey knowing what is expected of him while also feeling your love for him.

To be sure, effective communication with the nonassertive child requires much patience and persistence. Often it takes several attempts to open up the channels of communication. And if you're an assertive person yourself, you must be careful not to close off those channels by dominating the conversation. Still, even though communicating with a nonassertive child may require more time and effort than communicating with an assertive child, remember that the extra time and effort can yield huge dividends.

2. Communicating with the assertive child.

First, be prepared for the *when* and the *where* to be anytime and anyplace! Take a look at the two figures connected by the horizontal line on page 127. Again, the one on the right represents a parent, and the one on the left represents a child who is anything but shy. In fact, she wears her feelings on her sleeve. She's not afraid to talk to her parents and often initiates conversation. This is why the vertical line in this diagram is beside the parent, rather than the child. She doesn't need anyone to "draw her out." Instead, she usually seeks them out whenever she needs to talk about something.

My daughter, Beth, was an assertive child. I didn't have to worry about her coming to me—at least not when she was young. She always came to me—and Carol—whenever she had something on her mind. You might say that she was "in my face" whenever she needed to talk. Though she often came to me to ask a favor, she also came just to talk or share a problem.

Like Beth, most assertive children are "initiators" when it comes to everyday conversation. They're eager to talk—often at inopportune times. Let's reconsider the scenario of Carol and me talking in the kitchen, this time with Beth pulling on my pant leg. "Go away, Beth, can't you see I'm talking to your mother?" I would say. "Come back in ten minutes." Unlike Curt, who might not have come back at all, Beth would be back in only five minutes! I later learned that instead of sending her away for another five minutes, we should have stopped talking and given her our undivided attention. Though an assertive child is less easily discouraged than a nonassertive child, it *is* possible to eventually discourage the assertive child; and once you do, he or she will quit coming back to you as well. So, although your assertive child will initiate much of your communication, it is still very important for you to remain

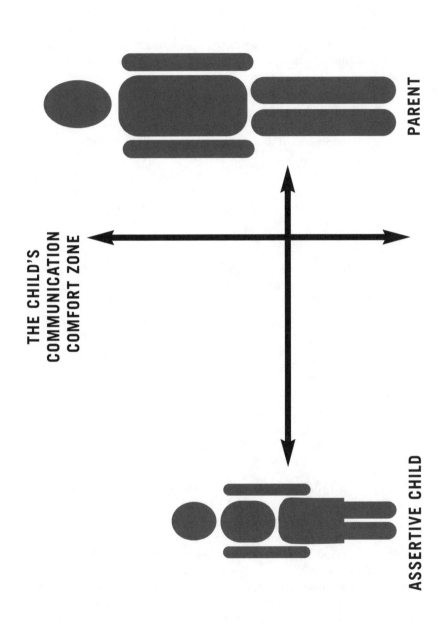

THE CHILD'S
COMMUNICATION
COMFORT ZONE

PARENT

ASSERTIVE CHILD

accessible. Although you probably won't have to be as intentional about daily communication with your assertive child as you might need to be with a nonassertive child, that everyday communication is equally important. Likewise, you will want to plan for an extended time of communication with your assertive child each week.

Although your assertive child often will initiate conversation, there will be times, obviously, when you will be the one initiating communication—particularly when the discussion is about a serious or sensitive issue. In these instances, you will find that assertive children are no different from nonassertive children: They are more approachable when they're in their comfort zones. Whenever I had something important to talk to Beth about, I knew I needed to meet her in her comfort zone. And, like Curt, her comfort zone happened to be her bedroom. We need to remember, then, that even assertive children are more attentive and receptive when they feel at ease.

Second, remember that the *how* is equally important when talking with an assertive child. Children are children, regardless of the manner in which they express themselves. Despite outward appearances, assertive children have the same emotions and sensitive feelings on the inside as nonassertive children do. They, too, need to be reassured that we love and care for them. Sometimes we tend to wear "kid gloves" when communicating with our nonassertive children and "boxing gloves" when communicating with our assertive children! So, while we're taking off those boxing gloves, we need to remember to take off our "sunglasses" as well. In other words, it's equally important for us to try to see things through the eyes of our assertive child and be intentional about expressing our love and care for that child. Again, I'll say more about this later in the chapter.

3. Communicating with your child.

As you can see, there are similarities in communicating effectively with both assertive and nonassertive children—being accessible, spending time together on a regular basis, meeting them in their comfort zones, seeing things from their perspective, expressing our love and care. Even so, because every child is a unique individual, we must pay close attention to each child's unique differences. As I have learned from coaching children in sporting events, we should never assume that a child's behavior in one situation clearly identifies how the child approaches communication. For example, I have seen children be assertive or aggressive on the ball field and yet be nonassertive when it comes to talking. Therefore, the categories we use to describe our children's personalities—compliant, strong-willed, and rebel—do not always correspond to their communication styles. A child can actually be compliant in behavior and yet assertive in communication. Likewise, a strong-willed child can be assertive in behavior and yet nonassertive when it comes to verbal communication. To complicate things even more, every child is a complex human being with ever-changing needs. Sometimes a child simply wants someone to listen and give a hug. Other times that same child needs more assertive feedback or requests. So, if you have concluded that communicating with children can be a confusing and difficult venture, you're right. It's not a lost cause, however! All it takes is a little observation and the willingness to adapt your approach to meet the needs of *your unique child.* I like to illustrate this point by contrasting the way Curt and Beth would come home after a date and the way Carol responded.

Let me set the stage. Our house has a big, heavy oak door in the front. When it is shut, the entire house shakes. We also have hardwood floors and steps leading to the upstairs bedrooms. Carol and I sleep with our bedroom door open and a small dog between us. Our dog has great hearing and a bark that pierces the soul. Besides the front door, there are several other doors leading into the house, and each of these doors is much smaller and lighter than the front door. We also have a carpeted staircase in the back of the house, leading to the upstairs bedrooms.

Now, how do you think Curt entered the house and got up to his bedroom without waking up the dog and us? You guessed it. He used a side door and the carpeted staircase. He knew that if he woke up the dog, then his mother might wake up and meet him at the top of the stairs. And he knew that she might ask him those horrible questions. You know the ones: "Did you have a good time? Did you kiss her goodnight? Are you going to ask her out again?" Now, to be fair to Carol, she might not have asked those questions, but Curt wasn't going to take a chance. The only way we would have known that Curt was home was if we had walked down the hall, opened his door, and looked inside his room.

Beth, on the other hand, was a different story. How do you think she entered the house? That's right: through the front door. The door would close with a loud "bam!" Then she would clomp up the hardwood stairs in her high heels. By then the dog would be barking like crazy and running around in circles on the bed. And often, especially if something exciting had happened on her date and she couldn't wait to share the news, she would come into our bedroom and shout, "Is anybody up?" I would quickly grab the dog by the throat and hold her under the covers with me. Carol, however, would perk right up and tell Beth that she was awake. Then Beth would sit on the bed next to her mom and talk and talk and talk.

Because of Carol's acute sensitivity to her children's styles, she never felt the need to meet Curt at the top of the stairs. She always knew that there would be plenty of other opportunities to talk to Curt. She always respected those times when Curt just simply didn't want to discuss an issue or even have small talk with his parents. Likewise, even those nights when she was awakened by Beth's noise and really wanted to go back to sleep, she always respected Beth's need to share a part of her life at that very moment. Carol always knew the time would come when Beth would not be coming home anymore, and she wanted to treasure those moments while she could. Because of my blindness to the rewards of being an effective communicator with our children, I, on the other hand, would get angry for being awakened from a sound sleep.

Please, please, please pay close attention to the unique communication styles and preferences of your children and make adjustments as necessary to meet each child's needs.

PARENT POINT
Improving Communication in Your Home

1. Recognize that children have different communication styles, and be adaptable in order to meet each child's needs.

---

2. Increase and optimize everyday communication opportunities with all family members (mealtimes, morning/bedtime routines, car time, phone calls, shared activities, etc.). Keep a log of daily one-on-one conversation time for one week and try to increase your conversation time with each family member. (See p. 142.)

3. Have an extended "one-on-one" (at least one hour) with every member of the family once a week.

4. Meet your child in his or her comfort zone (often the child's bedroom) for serious or meaningful conversations. Remember to give advance warning and turn off distractions such as radios and televisions.

5. Be accessible to your children and listen when they want to tell you something.

6. Try to save meaningful conversations with your spouse, or another adult, until after the children have gone to bed.

7. Practice attentive listening by acknowledging and naming your child's feelings, translating what your child is saying, and observing your child's body language. (See p. 135.)

8. Penetrate your child's feelings by practicing the skill of lightly probing, which is asking questions in a gentle, nonthreatening way. (See pp. 135-36.)

9. Stay on the "inside" of your children's lives by always listening, watching, and waiting. Encourage and allow them to express their true feelings.

10. Remember to take off your "sunglasses" so that you may express your love and care for the other person. (See pp. 139-41.)

11. Have weekly family meetings, followed by a fun family activity. (See pp. 143-44.)

12. Set aside one hour for a family quiet time each week (no mechanical noise allowed). Remember, you must remain attentive to the desires of the children. (See pp. 142-43.)

Stop Being an Ineffective Listener

After you've taken the first step toward improved communication in your home by recognizing you must adapt your approach to meet the needs of each child, you're ready to take the next and most difficult step: changing the way you communicate. This is necessary because, unfortunately, most of us are ineffective listeners.

As I learned in a college psychology class, human behavior is driven by needs. A famous researcher Abraham Maslow identified what became known as the Hierarchy of Needs. According to Maslow, the highest ranked needs that drive our behavior are food, shelter/safety, and clothing. Stephen Covey has suggested that once these basic needs are met, our next need is to be understood. It is this critical need related to communication, he says, that drives our behavior. One of his famous "habits" is "Seek first to understand and then to be understood." This simple and logical phrase, however, is very difficult to follow.

When you think about it, Covey makes wonderful sense. Someone begins to tell you something, and within the first few seconds of the conversation, your brain begins to build a response. You see, you both have a very high need to be understood. As human beings, we all have this need. So, before we can become good listeners, we must reprogram our brains, and this requires recognizing those bad behaviors that keep us from learning to understand before being understood.

The Hazelden company has identified several "problem personalities" we often assume when our children bring a problem to our attention. The first personality is called the "Drill Sergeant." The Drill Sergeant doesn't care what the child has to say. He simply barks out orders. We tend to become the Drill Sergeant when our children bring a problem to us and this problem makes us angry.

Instead of learning how the child feels and helping the child deal with the problem, we simply command the child to take a certain action. We make no effort to understand the child or to bring comfort.

The second personality is called the "Prosecuting Attorney." When we become the Prosecuting Attorney, we ask a number of aggressive and penetrating questions, trying to determine if the child is at fault. Our questions tell the child that he or she is at fault. Like the Drill Sergeant, we don't care about the feelings of the child, and we don't take time to understand.

The third personality is the "Psychiatrist." Before the child has a chance to tell her story, the Psychiatrist makes the mistake of telling the child how she feels and why she has these feelings. Very quickly the child realizes that her feelings don't count.

Other personalities include the "Comedian," the "Egomaniac," and the "Avoider." As the Comedian, we make fun of the situation. As the Egomaniac, we shift the focus from the child to ourselves. And as the Avoider, we change the subject or leave the room. Many times we assume these personalities because we have on our "sunglasses." For example, when our daughter doesn't make the team but her friend does, we remember that we, too, didn't make the team in our youth and we had hoped to relive the situation through our daughter. On the other hand, if our daughter makes the team, then we make it, too. Our "sunglasses" can also cause us to make light of a problem because it reminds us of a similar problem we had when we were young that we don't want to relive. All of these personality types keep us from being good listeners and effective communicators with our children. When we assume these personalities with a nonassertive child, we run the risk that the child will quit sharing his or her feelings. When we assume these personalities with an assertive child, we run the risk that the child will find another person to share his or her feelings with.

In addition to these "problem personalities," there are several ineffective listening habits that can keep us from being effective communicators with our children, as Stephen Covey identifies in his book *The 7 Habits of Highly Effective Families*. Regrettably, I perfected two of these poor listening habits and came terribly close to passing them on to my children.

The first one is called "selective listening." I refined this listening technique at the office. As my company reduced the size of its workforce without reducing the amount of work that needed to be done, I and many other managers had to become more efficient. I discovered that one way to accomplish this goal was to spend less time talking with my employees. I listened when a subject being discussed was high on my priority list or interested me personally. Otherwise, I ignored what was being said. I became so accustomed to selective listening that I began doing it at home, too. I listened and contributed to the discussion whenever my family talked about sports or other subjects that interested me, but I "tuned out" whenever they discussed a subject that was boring to me or made me feel uncomfortable. Since Beth hated sports, we didn't talk very much.

The other ineffective listening technique is called "pretend listening." I also refined this bad habit at the office. When my employees came into my office, it was easier to merely pretend to listen to them while I continued doing my own work. Again, I found that what worked well at the office also worked well at home. This was all well and good until my family began to imitate my bad listening habits. You see, they had learned that I was both a selective listener and a pretend listener with them, so they began to be both selective and pretend listeners with me. I had only myself to blame.

The good news is that we don't have to pass bad listening habits on to our children. Instead, we can teach them good listening habits by modeling those habits ourselves. If we want to become effective communicators, we must learn to be the best listeners we can be.

Start Becoming an Effective Listener

Our goal as parents should be to become *effective listeners*—or active listeners, as some experts put it. According to Covey, this is the highest level of listening. It involves attentive listening and a skill he calls lightly probing. Without the skill of lightly probing, we never rise above the level of attentive listening. So, let's consider these two skills necessary for effective listening, along with two additional skills I believe are equally important to being effective listeners as parents.

1. An effective listener practices attentive listening.

An effective listener is first and foremost an attentive listener. Attentive listening is critical when a child is upset and feelings are out in the open. In their book *How to Talk to Kids So Kids Will Listen & Listen So Kids Will Talk,* Adele Faber and Elaine Mazlish give some practical suggestions for becoming an attentive listener. First, they recommend that we listen quietly, acknowledging our children's feelings with simple words such as, "Oh, I see." In addition, they suggest we give our children's feelings a name, such as saying, "That sounds frustrating," or "That must make you feel sad." They caution us to avoid making unhelpful responses such as blaming or accusing; giving threats, warnings, or commands; moralizing; making comparisons; and using sarcasm. If we want to elicit cooperation from our children, we must simply acknowledge their feelings rather than tell them we know how they feel. It's also helpful to translate what our children are saying, rather than interpret the information. I tell parents to restate in another way what their children are saying as if they are translating what their children are saying from one language into another. When we translate, we don't wear our "sunglasses"—our preconceived ideas and views shaped by our experience. We actually *hear* every word.

As I've mentioned, a good place to practice attentive listening is in your child's room. Whenever you go to your child's room to talk, insist on turning off the radio, TV, and other mechanical noises. Then *really listen* to what your child is saying as you acknowledge and name your child's feelings, translate what your child is saying, and observe your child's body language. Experts claim that children under the age of ten communicate 80 percent of the time through body language. So, part of attentive listening is paying close attention to body language—both your child's and your own. This includes maintaining good eye contact. Remember, in order to give your child the best advice you can give, you must become an attentive listener and truly pay attention to every aspect of your child's verbal and nonverbal communication.

2. An effective listener lightly probes.

An effective listener also practices a skill called lightly probing. The Drill Sergeant knows how to probe, as does the Prosecuting

Attorney. Unfortunately, neither one does it *lightly*. Lightly probing is simply asking questions in a gentle, nonthreatening way. Lightly probing takes away some of the layers that are keeping the child's feeling from coming to the surface. For example, the child comes home from school and his body language is telling you that he had a bad day. When you ask him what kind of day he had, he responds, "okay." Instead of accepting his first response, you ask him to tell you about the activities he did at school today. You ask him about his friends or a certain course. One of the advantages of lightly probing is that it keeps the conversation from ending.

Lightly probing is particularly helpful when you are dealing with a shy child, because it allows you to penetrate into the child's deeper feelings. Lightly probing helps you to clarify the type of feelings your child has. Lightly probing keeps you from telling your child how *you* would feel if you were in your child's shoes, and thus "taking away" your child's feelings. In other words, lightly probing keeps the focus on your child, where it should be.

3. An effective listener stays on the "inside."

A third skill, or habit, critical to all parents who want to be effective listeners is what I call staying on the "inside." Though I had hoped to be a different kind of dad, one who was "in the loop," I really didn't know how to listen, and, consequently, I was rarely on the "inside" of my children's lives. This diagram illustrates my problem.

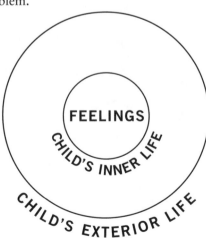

The outside circle represents what I call my children's exterior lives, which I compare to the earth's surface or crust. The smaller circle on the inside represents my children's inner lives, which I compare to the earth's core. As you can see in the diagram, their feelings are contained within their inner lives, their inner selves, just as hot magma or lava is contained within the earth's core. My ineffective listening style always kept me on the outside, the exterior. From time to time, however, my children's feelings would come gushing out, just as hot lava comes gushing out from inside the earth whenever there is an eruption. Because I knew neither the root cause of the eruption nor how to respond to their feelings, I programmed myself to react the same way each time an "eruption" would occur. I would get angry and either shout at them or belittle their feelings. "Come on, it's time for you to grow up," I'd say. Their anger always seemed to fuel my own anger.

It seems I'm not alone. Many fathers have told me that their children's emotional eruptions often seem to stem from something insignificant—at least from their point of view—and thus they don't want to spend any time dealing with the issue. It seems that most men don't like wasting time dealing with what we perceive to be "insignificant" issues. Over the years, this tactic ends up being a lose/lose situation for us. First, we lose with our children, and, second, we lose with our wives.

Women, on the other hand, tend to be more effective in staying on the inside. Carol was no exception. Why? She *enjoyed* listening. She wasn't afraid of being exposed to our children's messy or complicated or painful emotions. In fact, she welcomed it. When Curt was young, she even bought a parenting book to help her learn to express her displeasure with him appropriately. She also was *intentional* about listening. She made herself available. She spent time with the children. She was with them at breakfast and at dinner. She helped them with their homework after school. She even watched television with them. And because both Curt and Beth participated in various activities, she spent lots of time in the car with them. Whether they were traveling to one of Curt's many tennis tournaments or one of Beth's dance competitions or somewhere else, she would take advantage of the opportunity to listen to them.

When we were living in Spartanburg and Curt was having such a hard time making friends, we sent him by plane to space camp in

Huntsville, Alabama. At the conclusion of the camp, Curt sounded so excited about the experience that Carol decided to drive to Huntsville and bring Curt back herself. "You're crazy!" I exclaimed. "All those miles!" On the way home, Curt never stopped talking. Carol loved every minute of their conversation, and so did Curt. When they got home and I asked Curt how he liked the camp, he simply said, "It was okay," and gave me a commercial tape of the camp. Carol had known that Curt would be eager and willing to talk in the car, and she didn't want to miss this experience.

Since Carol spent so much time on the "inside" of her children's lives—close to their true feelings—she never overreacted to their emotional eruptions. Instead, she embraced them. She knew that they were coming, that it was just a matter of time. She knew because she was on the inside—listening, watching, and waiting. Let me illustrate with an example of a typical episode in our family.

Let's say that Beth had an argument with her girlfriend. She told Carol about it, but not me. A few days later, Beth suddenly exploded in anger when she heard we were having one of her least favored meals for dinner. I'm caught completely off guard, and I overreact. Carol, on the other hand, embraces the anger because she has been waiting for it to come out. (Does any of this sound familiar?) She knew that Beth's response to the fight with her best friend had been too controlled.

We want our children to share their innermost feelings with us, and yet sometimes we react in such a negative manner that our children feel it's safer to keep their feelings inside. No matter how angry or frustrated they can make us feel by sharing the truth with us, we are always far better off when our children feel they can share their true feelings with us. Staying on the "inside" of our children's lives means learning to be effective listeners, and one of the many rewards of being effective listeners is always being on the inside of our children's lives. Although it is time-consuming, it is definitely rewarding.

I'll always regret the many long nights I spent at the office and the many dinners I ate by myself. Please, please, please spend as much time with your children as you can and learn to enjoy being on the "inside."

4. *An effective listener takes off her or his "sunglasses."*

One of the concepts I emphasize throughout this book is that we tend to view the world through our "sunglasses," which are all the life experiences that have shaped our existence. Looking at the world through our life experiences, however, makes effective listening a very difficult task! This is why it is so important for us to remember to take off our sunglasses when we're talking with others— especially with our family members. Wearing our sunglasses prevents us from seeing things through others' eyes. Wearing our sunglasses keeps our focus on ourselves rather than on others. Wearing our sunglasses, then, makes it very difficult to express our love and care for others. As we considered earlier in the chapter, we often wear our sunglasses with our children when we "give them the third degree" by presenting a series of questions or when we express our feelings before giving them a chance to express theirs. We take off our sunglasses by intentionally expressing our genuine love and care for our children through our words (using attentive listening and lightly probing), our body language, and our actions.

I'd like to share two stories that illustrate the importance of taking our sunglasses off in order to become effective communicators with our children. The first is about Curt. After he went off to college, he called to talk to Carol several times a week. Instead of seeing things through Curt's eyes, I kept my sunglasses on and saw his phone calls as an expression of a preference for his mother. One day I had an emotional eruption and screamed at Carol, "Why don't you let him grow up, Carol? He is in college, and it is time that you cut the cord." On the inside, however, I was saying, "Why, Curt, don't you ever call me?"

The second story is about Beth. When she was a freshman in college, Beth had a fight with her boyfriend. As usual, I took her side and was very angry at the young man. Every day Carol and Beth talked. As our phone bill skyrocketed, so did my anger. I wanted to tell Beth that this guy was a jerk and it was a good thing she had found that out now instead of later. However, I had begun the process of seeing the world through her eyes, and so I kept my mouth shut. One night the phone rang just after 10:00 P.M. Because I start my bedtime routine at 10:00 P.M. (I have ice cream and gingersnaps while watching a syndicated TV drama with my dog, Winston, by my side, sharing the goodies), I let Carol answer any late calls. That night, however, she was out of town. And something inside of me told me to answer the phone. It was Beth, and she quickly asked if her mom was home. I had a choice to make. I could give her the phone number of Carol's hotel, or I could tell her that I was ready to listen. God told me to tell Beth that I was there to listen. For the next thirty minutes, she cried on the phone. She told me how angry she was. Once again I had the great urge to tell her that she was very lucky to find out now what a lousy person her boyfriend was. Instead, I took off my sunglasses, which were keeping me from expressing my love and care for Beth, and I kept my mouth shut. Occasionally I reinforced something she said or I lightly probed by asking a question. When she was finished talking, she said, "Thanks, Dad. I love you." When I hung up the phone, I cried like a baby. I had passed the test. Finally, I had been able to be there for my daughter. Learning how to listen to your children with your sunglasses off is a great and rewarding achievement. (By the way, Beth forgave the boy and they got back together!)

Besides wearing our sunglasses when communicating with our children, we often wear our sunglasses when communicating with our spouses. Sometimes that's an even greater challenge. Though Carol was always an attentive listener with the children, even when they would have an emotional eruption, she couldn't take off her sunglasses when I was the one having the emotional eruption! You see, as a child, Carol always had trouble dealing with the anger of others; this is why she automatically reacted negatively to me whenever I raised my voice.

In my parenting classes, I like to have a little fun describing what would happen whenever I lost my temper around Carol. First, Carol would get a can of gasoline, and, just as she was about to pour the gasoline over me, she would exclaim, "Jim, you are overreacting!" I would scream back at her, "I am not overreacting!" She then would go to the kitchen drawer and get a pack of matches. Just before she would light the gasoline, she would exclaim, "Now you are being defensive!" Poof! I would go up in smoke and look like Beetle Bailey after the Sarge had beaten him up!

Instead of being able to listen attentively and understand my feelings, Carol couldn't keep from looking through her sunglasses and remembering the difficult times she had as child. Once I finally realized this, I tried much harder not to lose my temper around her. And whenever I did, I would apologize more quickly instead of wondering what the "big deal" was all about.

So, in addition to remembering that we need to take off our own sunglasses, we need to remember that sometimes our spouses may have difficulty taking off their sunglasses because of difficulties or even emotional scars from the past. At those times, it's wise to remember that the measure we give is the measure we will get!

PARENT POINT
Helping Your Child to Understand You

1. Always try to maintain a pleasant, respectful tone of voice.

2. Be aware of your body language. For example, avoid crossing your arms, and always maintain good eye contact.

3. After expressing your feelings or giving your input, ask your child to repeat back what you just said.

4. Give examples to illustrate the point you are trying to make.

5. Remember that the younger the child, the shorter his or her attention span. If you're starting to lose a younger child's attention, try being a little more animated.

6. Never dominate the conversation; let your child know that you truly want to hear what he or she has to say.

7. Encourage and allow respectful discussion and debate. However, whenever core values are in question, reinforce your point of view by making references and connections to your family's value system or mission statement. In time, your child will come to realize that there are certain issues that are nonnegotiable.

8. Create an environment of love, trust, and support in your home.

Three Great Ways to Improve Communication in Your Family Now

In addition to the specific communication skills I've suggested throughout this chapter, there are three ideas I urge all parents to try. If you do, I am confident you will realize *immediate* benefits!

1. Keep a conversation log for one week.

As you recall, we learned in chapter 2 that the average parent spends only fifteen minutes a day per child having a one-on-one conversation. That's why I urge parents to keep a conversation log for one week. Nothing will motivate you to spend more time talking with your children than realizing how little time you actually spend talking with them on a daily basis. Here's how it works. Keep a piece of paper and a pencil on the nightstand and, before going to bed each night, recall the number of minutes you spent talking with each child that day. If you have trouble estimating this, then you might want to keep a small notepad handy throughout the day and make a notation after each one-on-one conversation. You will want to note both the total number of minutes per child as well as the total number of minutes spent saying something *positive* to each child. This may seem tedious at first, but you'll soon find yourself paying close attention to your conversations—which, after all, is the whole point of the exercise! If the actual time is lower than what the children need or lower than what you'd like it to be, then identify steps you can take to increase the time you spend communicating with each of your children. Although I recommend you keep the log for only one week, you may find it beneficial to repeat the exercise periodically as a "checkup."

2. Have a family quiet time each week.

In my opinion, one of the best recommendations Stephen Covey makes in his book *The 7 Habits of Highly Effective Families* is to have a regular quiet time each week. Basically, this means that sometime between Monday and Thursday you set aside one hour for a time of quiet activity. I recommend that families try to do this on the same day and at the same time each week for continuity. As I define it, quiet time simply means no mechanical noise is allowed. Some families like this idea so much that they have one hour of quiet time each night! During this hour, the parents must be attentive to the desires of the children. One mom came back to class after trying this with her family and told me that her husband was very angry with me. The husband had mistakenly thought that the quiet time would give him a chance to read the paper. Instead, his four-year-old came and sat on his lap, and she talked to him for the entire hour. Mom was extremely pleased, and, truth be told, I'll bet Dad was too!

3. Have regular family meetings.

There was a time in my life when my inability to handle stress was causing me to be angry and disconnected from my family much of the time. One day my therapist suggested that I hold family meetings on a weekly basis to improve the unity of the family. So, when I got home that afternoon, I announced that we were going to have a family meeting the following night. Everyone was required to attend. Prior to the meeting, I made out my list of complaints. I even had a sublist for each member of the family. By the time the family had gathered around the coffee table, I was ready. One by one, I went through my checklist. When I was finished, I asked if anyone had anything they wanted to discuss. They all said no. My therapist had said that the meeting should not be longer than one hour, so I was very proud that it had taken only fifteen minutes. I also felt better because I had gotten so many things off my chest. Just as I was ready to leave the room, I felt the presence of two "daggers" ready to be launched. I turned around, and there stood Carol. She looked upset. She said, "Boy, that was a lot of fun. I can't wait to have another one." Then she stomped out of the room. I am not sure if we ever had another family meeting.

Years later, Covey's book taught me the correct way to have a family meeting. First of all, keep in mind that a family meeting is a time for teaching and planning and keeping track of one another's activities; it is not a time for complaining or criticizing. It's important to choose a time when everyone will be together, and to give each family member a chance to talk. (I suggest holding family meetings after church. After all, aren't we at peace when we leave church?) Prior to the meeting, determine who will chair the meeting (have family members take turns from week to week), and have this person create the agenda by interviewing family members and asking for their input. Of course, a parent should help a young child with this. As with most families, sometimes our togetherness generates disagreements. When this happens, it is up to us, as parents, to mediate and to seek a compromise that all family members can accept. One helpful hint is to limit the meeting to one hour. If your family has a difficult time finding compromises, then few subjects will be covered. Feedback from families who hold regular family meetings suggests that there will always be some bumps in the road, but over time, the road will smooth out. Finally, I recommend that the chairperson end the meeting with a prayer, thanking God for the many blessings of your family.

I also recommend that you plan to do some kind of family activity after every family meeting. Particularly if the mediation during the meeting did not go as smoothly as you had hoped, another family activity will help to bring everyone back together. This activity also will give you an opportunity to praise your children for their involvement in the meeting. Having a meal together is the most popular activity.

Please, please, please make improving the communication in your family a top priority, beginning today. If you do, you will not only build stronger relationships, but you also will create a more loving and peaceful home environment.

QUESTIONS TO PONDER

1. Have you identified the communication style of each family member?

2. Where are the comfort zones of each of your children?

3. If you have an assertive child, what steps do you need to take

in order to keep from wearing your "boxing gloves" when communicating with this child?

4. What steps do you need to take in order to ensure that you don't wear your "sunglasses" when communicating with family members?

5. What have you learned from keeping your communication log for one week?

6. Which of the "problem personalities" do you find yourself assuming most often when communicating with your children?

9

HANDLING ANGER IN A
POSITIVE WAY

Scripture Link

*A fool gives full vent to . . . anger, but a wise [person]
keeps himself [or herself] under control.*
—*Proverbs 29:11 NIV*

Those who are wise will calm anger.
—*Proverbs 29:8b NLT*

*Do not be overcome by evil, but overcome evil with
good.* —*Romans 12:21 NIV*

I have a doctoral degree in anger. I don't have a diploma or a
fancy robe, but I have enough personal experience with anger
to make me astute in the subject; and it seems as if I've spent
enough money on counseling to have paid my way through grad-
uate school! For you to understand the sources of my anger, you
need to know my story. All of us who have a problem with anger
have at least one story. Perhaps you do, too. Unfortunately, it
took me a long time to understand that my stories never justified
my anger. It also took me a long time to understand that uncontrolled anger, which leads to verbal or physical violence, requires
professional help. My intent in this chapter is twofold: (1) to help
you reduce the anger and conflict in your home, and (2) to help
you identify if you or someone in your family may have a more
serious problem with anger and need to seek professional help.
In either case, there's good news: We *can* learn to control our
anger.

My Personal Struggle with Anger

My "story" began on a day in 1983 when I bent over to pick up a log for the fireplace and felt a twinge in my back. Within a few short months, that twinge became constant pain. I could not sit for more than one hour or stand in place for more than ten minutes. I was X-rayed from top to bottom, and no problem could be found. Then, in 1985, the best doctors in Pittsburgh decided that the muscle spasms I was having must be caused by a problem with a disk in my lower back. They operated on the disk, but the pain didn't cease. In fact, my pain worsened after the operation. To make matters worse, at that time I was starting a new job in Spartanburg, South Carolina. The job was a promotion, an award for all my hard work, and yet I couldn't sit or stand. I interviewed my employees while lying in a lounge chair. Everyone wanted to work for me!

Before long, I was working ten- to twelve-hour days, as well as most Saturdays and a few Sundays. When the pain would get to be too much for me to handle, I would close my office door and work on the floor. Eventually my staff got used to this and would actually join me on the floor! At night I would lie in bed and take muscle relaxers in order to sleep. Finally, the pain got so bad that I couldn't get out of bed. My wife came to my rescue by talking to a chiropractor. In time, this practitioner got me out of bed and into a program at the YMCA. Each night after work I walked laps in the pool. Eventually, my muscles regained strength, and I was able to become more active. I was told that my back pain would be with me for the rest of my life. As I became more and more active, I began to think that I could handle this life sentence.

As anyone who has suffered from chronic pain knows, pain can lead to feelings of anger. My back pain was the initial source of my anger. On my worst days, I thought I was entitled to my anger. It was my friend. It became a part of me just like an arm or a leg. I took it with me everywhere, including work and home.

In addition to my back pain, my new job required me to endure verbal abuse. Though I rarely lost my temper at the office, I was absorbing a tremendous amount of negative stimuli from my supervisors. I learned all too well that bullies exist in the corporate world, too. The few times I responded in kind, I was almost fired.

To me, being on the receiving end of verbal abuse was like someone was kicking me in the back. I was storing this negative energy deep inside; but, like a pressure cooker, I had to have a release valve. So, the "steam" would come out each evening in my home. This steam was the verbal violence that came out of my mouth directed to my family.

During those long eight years, I kept asking God to take away my back pain. That didn't happen. Looking back on those years, I now know that my prayers were misguided. I should have asked God to give me the strength to learn how to handle all the negative stimuli in my life in a more positive way. Finally, God helped me to realize that I needed professional help—that my anger was destroying not only my life, but also the life of my family. Carol had wanted me to get help for a long time, and finally I agreed. I started working with a wonderful licensed therapist on a weekly basis, and I found these sessions to be very helpful. She helped me to see that I had "crossed the line" with my anger by allowing my words and actions to attack the person, instead of addressing the person's behavior.

As I got better at handling my negative feelings without crossing the line with my children or my wife, God once again held out a helping hand. Another subsidiary of the parent company needed accounting assistance. They hired me as a consultant. I quickly rediscovered the love that comes from doing something you like with people who are kind and appreciative. A year later, I was asked to be the controller. Although it would mean a decrease in pay, I jumped at the opportunity. In addition to exchanging a verbally abusive environment for a group of supportive people, I was able to significantly reduce the number of hours I was working overtime. Much to my surprise, my back pain diminished, and I began to understand that stress also had been contributing to my pain.

With my therapy going well, my job going well, and my anger decreasing, things were beginning to turn around. Then, tragedy struck. Curt was killed by a drunk driver. Six months later, the subsidiary closed, and I was fired by the parent company for not being willing to transfer to Texas. Now I was facing new sources of negative energy, and I had to decide if I was going to once again become a pressure cooker, releasing my "steam" at home.

Thankfully, I was able to avoid repeating that cycle and, instead, learn to control my anger and release it in positive ways. In the remainder of this chapter, I offer the most beneficial information that has helped me to do just that—information I have gained through a variety of excellent counselors and many years of research. It is my hope that this information will be helpful to you, as well. However, because I realize that the concepts and techniques that worked for me may not hold all the "answers" for you, I share this information in the hope that it will become a catalyst in your life to seek even more practical knowledge and help.

Understanding the Difference
Between Anger and Rage

Now, as I look back on that angry period in my life with the benefit of knowledge gained through professional counseling and study, I recognize the many mistakes I made—mistakes such as thinking that I was entitled to "keep" my anger, nursing my anger instead of turning it over to God, believing that my anger couldn't harm my family, and staying so many years with a company that tolerated verbal abuse. But perhaps the biggest mistake of all was thinking that my problem was anger when, actually, my problem was rage. As I later learned, there is a big difference between anger and rage. Unfortunately, our society has forgotten this distinction and has chosen to use the word *anger* almost exclusively. Understanding the difference is paramount to understanding how to cope with your negative feelings in a positive way.

Anger is displeasure resulting from injury, mistreatment, or opposition. It is a normal human emotion that everyone experiences. Many times anger stems from situations surrounding things or people that you care about deeply. Although anger is negative energy, it can and should be released in positive ways. When we do not find positive ways to release our anger, allowing the negative energy to build within us, our anger turns into rage.

Rage, then, is uncontrolled anger. It is the negative release of negative energy. It is synonymous with violence, both verbal and physical. Rage occurs when you "cross the line." Rage occurs when you verbally attack the person instead of the behavior. Rage also occurs when you use physical violence against someone else. I

149

believe it is a sin to allow anger to become rage. Unfortunately, the entertainment industry conveys the message that violence is okay and should be respected as a good way to solve problems. The truth, however, is that rage is evil because it does harm to others and pulls you away from your path. And, if left unchecked, it can even cause destruction—to individuals, to relationships, and to families.

Handling Your Anger—Before It Turns to Rage

The key to handling anger—and, thus, preventing rage—is learning how to release negative feelings in a positive way. Instead of merely learning how to handle our children's anger—which seems to be the emphasis of many parenting books—we must learn to handle our own anger first. All behavior is learned through example. This means that our children learn how to behave—or not to behave—by modeling our behavior.

So, how do we learn to handle our anger in a positive way?

1. Learn to pause.

Of all the information I've gathered, I've found that one of the most basic concepts is also one of the most helpful. It is simply learning to pause. In his book *The 7 Habits of Highly Effective Families,* Stephen Covey reminds us that every stimulus we receive generates a response, and what separates us from the animals is that God has given us the ability to pause. When God created us, he gave us certain gifts to help us pause—gifts such as self-awareness, a conscience, free will, and a sense of humor. Unfortunately, many times we forget to pause, and we allow our anger to become rage. Simply remembering to pause is one of the most powerful methods of keeping our negative stimulus in control.

The concept of a pause button is certainly not new. For generations, mothers around the world have been practicing the simple method of counting to ten. My own mother was a nursery school teacher, and she used this technique both at school and at home. She didn't just count silently; no, she counted out loud so that everyone could hear! My siblings and I rarely saw Mom get angry; but when we heard her begin counting out loud, the last thing any of us wanted was for her to reach the number ten! Whenever I was the guilty party, I would quickly recite my many excuses until she reached the number seven. By seven, I would realize that my excuses weren't working. Then I would switch to plan B, which was to tell her I was sorry and ask if she would forgive me. Even though there were times when I wasn't exactly sure what crime I had committed, I found it was safer to implement plan B whenever Mom reached number seven.

Counting to ten is a simple yet very effective way to release the negative energy of anger—or, to put it another way, to respond positively to the negative stimulus. During these ten seconds, you use the other gifts God has given you. For example, you make yourself become aware of your feelings. Those ten seconds give you a chance to choose your response, a chance to use your sense of humor or your imagination. I think my mom knew that because she was only human, she was capable of crossing the line with her children. She knew that as a human she was capable of punishing her children instead of giving us effective consequences. So, by counting to ten, she gave herself the opportunity to choose to use the gifts God had given her; and we kids got all the benefits.

Other people pause by walking away from the moment at hand. They might say, "Excuse me, child, but I can't talk to you right now about this behavior. I need time to calm down. I will get back to you later in the day and discuss your consequence." I have seen other adults take a deep breath and let out the air very slowly. People who are aware of the importance of handling their negative feelings in a constructive and healthy way know the importance of the pause.

2. Let it out.

There are times when we all need a more physical type of release. Whenever I'm doing a classroom presentation on handling anger, I always do this simple demonstration. I open a door, walk outside, and scream very loudly. This procedure always elicits laughter, but it's a serious example of a physical way to release anger. There are times when we just need to remove ourselves from the negative stimulus and let our feelings out.

When I was young, we had a punching bag in the basement. I

was taught to let out my anger by punching this bag or pounding the pillows in my room. My brother likes to run. While he burns calories, he also is releasing negative energy. Most people tell me that any kind of exercise helps them to release negative energy. I never liked to run, but I enjoyed swimming; and I learned that it is a wonderful release as well. Carol likes to walk the dog. Letting it out doesn't mean you have to scream; it means that you find some kind of "release value" in your life. I'll revisit this important step in just a moment when we talk specifically about ways to reduce the stress in your life.

3. Find something to laugh about.

As mentioned previously, a sense of humor is one of the gifts God gave us to help us pause before responding to a negative stimulus. Humor helps us to diffuse or lessen the intensity of our feelings. Sometimes humor acts as a pause button. Humor gives us the opportunity to choose a positive response to our negative feelings. Humor helps us not to cross the line with our family. I once knew a man, for example, who used humor to diffuse sticky situations with his wife. He was a laid-back kind of guy, and his wife was much more aggressive. Just when his wife was about ready to cross the line, he would jump into the air and say, "Baby, you are nipping at my heels!" She would burst out laughing, and the anger—both his and hers—would be diffused.

One day after telling this story in a class, a parent told me that he had tried the same approach but, instead of laughing, his wife had become very angry and had accused him of not caring about her feelings. What I have learned is that each person, or each couple, must find their own humor; and for certain situations and for certain individuals, humor is not always an appropriate response.

When Beth and I were at our worst, she thought that by shouting this phrase at me I would calm down: "Chill out, Dad!" Instead, the hair on the back of my neck would rise, and I would shout back, "I'm not getting angry, Beth!" Today, Beth simply whispers in my ear, "You're losing it, Dad." I always begin to laugh, and I'm able to vent my anger in a positive way. I am sure that there are several reasons why the new phrase works. First of all, she doesn't shout it at me! Second, she doesn't embarrass me in front of other people. And third, I am so much more at peace in her company today that my sense of humor is much stronger.

Of course, there are times when there's simply nothing funny in a particular situation. Even in such times, however, humor can be used in a delayed sense as a way to release pent up negative feelings. When one of my supervisors threatened me with bodily harm, humor did not come to my rescue. However, months later when I told the story to my friends and I acted out how my supervisor had behaved, demonstrating his facial expressions, we laughed together. This laughter helped me heal from a terrible hurt.

When I think of times when humor has enabled me to handle negative energy, I always think of my childhood. Remember that punching bag we had in the basement? Whenever someone gave one of us kids a hard time, we would draw the person's face on a piece of paper, attach it to the punching bag, and laugh ourselves silly while harmlessly punching away. I also had a dartboard, and whenever a girl would dump me, I would put her picture on the bull's eye and, well, you get the picture! These personal moments kept me from retaliating or from responding with hurtful remarks.

I've always been one of those funny people who make people laugh—even as a child. God gave me a quick wit and a good sense of humor. Whenever my family moved into a new neighborhood, it was never long before we were invited to a party. I was cheap entertainment! As an adult, I frequently used my sense of humor at work. Unfortunately, I rarely used it at home. This became very clear to me when my brother, Biff, came to visit us one year. I had been bringing home bushels of negative energy from work, and the children could not remember the last time they'd seen me smile. One night Biff started telling Curt and Beth stories about my childhood. He had everyone in hysterics, including me. It felt so good to laugh—really laugh—and to realize how much I needed laughter in my life.

We'd all do ourselves good to remember that, in most instances, a sense of humor and a little creativity can be very effective tools for diffusing anger.

4. Confide in someone.

Another important way to release anger is to share your feelings with someone you trust. I like to call this special someone a "soul mate." Every child and every adult needs to have a soul mate. As I define it, a soul mate is someone who is a good listener, someone who has no ownership of the problem you need to discuss, someone who can allow you to vent without being offended, and someone who translates the words he or she hears instead of interpreting them.

Generally speaking, spouses and siblings are not good choices because they often are involved in your day-to-day problems and can't be objective. Parents should help each child find a soul mate, although sometimes these relationships develop on their own. It happened that way for me. By the time I was in middle school, my aunt had become my soul mate. She was able to listen to me without taking ownership of the problem. Grandparents can be wonderful soul mates for children as well.

Because women are naturally more verbal, they seem to have an advantage over men when it comes to sharing their feelings. This is why most women naturally seek out a soul mate—a best friend—whom they can talk with intimately. Men, on the other hand, seem to hold their feelings in and have difficulty verbalizing their feelings to others. I realize that I have just stereotyped the entire world and that there are exceptions; my point is simply that most women do tend to be more open with their feelings than men and, therefore, more proactive in finding a soul mate. The truth is, however, that men need a soul mate just as much as women do. Contrary to what some men believe, it's not a "woman thing"!

Sometimes the church can help to "connect" individuals for the purpose of sharing and listening. Many churches train laypeople, called Stephen Ministers, to provide comfort and support to others. My mother has had the same Stephen Minister for almost ten years. During the final years of my dad's life, a time when his hearing was declining and he was easily confused, her Stephen Minister was a lifesaver. Instead of falling into the routine of analyzing or judging the information, this wonderful woman just listened to my mom and supported her emotionally. Now this woman is helping my mom deal with the loss of my father.

In addition to confiding in a soul mate, some people discover that joining a support group of individuals who can relate personally to a particular crisis or a continuing struggle can be very beneficial. After we lost Curt, a women's support group formed to help Carol, and a men's support group was started for me. Now, over six years later, Carol's group still meets every week. They have become soul mates for one another. They have helped one another deal with a lot of negative stimuli, including death, divorce, and disease. The men's support group, on the other hand, lasted only six months. One by one, the members dropped out. Perhaps it was coincidence, but every time one of the men would open up and share his deepest feelings, he would not return the following week. Meanwhile, my feelings were gushing out at every meeting, making the sessions very helpful to me personally. One individual did stay with me until the end, and he is still a friend today. My point is that many people—both women and men—find support groups to be a wonderful way of dealing with the negative stimuli in their lives in a positive manner.

5. Reduce your stress.

Stress is one of the most powerful catalysts for anger. I realized this truth when I finally was able to leave the company where I had been verbally abused and transfer to a much smaller company where the working atmosphere was kinder and more supportive. After accepting this new job, much to my surprise, I found that I was sleeping more soundly, feeling better physically, and having less back pain. I felt as if a huge burden had been lifted. As the stress decreased, so did my anger. Though Curt died shortly after I started this new job, I was better equipped emotionally to handle my grief because my stress level had already significantly decreased. Unfortunately, my new job lasted less than one year. The good news is that I promised myself that my next job would not be stressful but would be in sync with my personal goals. In other words, it would be a job that I could *enjoy!*

Perhaps you can relate. So many of the parents who attend my classes are under too much stress. They often tell me they don't sleep well, they don't like their jobs—or even their lives—and they get angry easily. Well, it's not surprising that you're more prone to get angry and lose your temper (rage) when you're not sleeping enough and you're stressed out at work and/or at home! So, what can you do about it?

1. Get enough sleep. Lack of sufficient sleep is one of the

primary causes of stress-induced rage. Most parents, unfortunately, refuse to take this fact seriously. They refuse to try an experiment in order to discover how much sleep they actually need. It's
very simple. For three straight days you go to bed when you are
tired, and you wake up when your body tells you it's time. (If necessary, do this over a long weekend, holiday break, or vacation.)
By the third day, you should have a good idea how many hours of
sleep you need. During these three days, it's important to try to be
as "stress free" as possible and avoid inhibitors such as caffeine
and alcohol. If you want to get a handle on your anger, start by
getting a handle on your sleep requirements. (By the way, the same
is true for children as well. I can tell you firsthand that the majority of students I see on a daily basis are not getting enough sleep.)

2. Prioritize. A simple time management exercise can help you
to eliminate much of the stress in your day-to-day life. First, list
everything requiring your time and attention. Second, rate each
item as an A, B, or C. The A's are most important, the B's are some-
what important, and the C's are least important. Third, ignore the
C's until they become B's. Fourth, establish a time line of completion for every B and A item. Now, focus your time and energy on
the A's. By the way, faith and family-related items should always
be A's!

Before I say more about prioritizing family, let me say a word
about faith. By faith, I mean your personal relationship with God.
Prioritizing your faith means regular devotional time, worshiping
on a weekly basis, attending Sunday school, and making a commitment to at least one other church group or committee. Though
your faith should always be an "A," sometimes even the church
can become a source of stress in our lives. I remember a mom in
one of my classes who cried in front of the group as she told us that
she had recently accepted her third committee assignment from her
church. We all prayed for her to find the strength to go back to the
church and talk to her minister about it. The following week she
cried again, but this time they were tears of joy. She not only
resigned from the latest committee, but she also resigned from one
other. The minister agreed that, at this point in her life, her family
needed more of her time, and the church members and God would
understand. My point in sharing this story is not to say that we
should stop participating in the life of the church; rather, we

should not allow our church involvement—or any other commitment outside the home—to compromise our family obligations and family values, which should include spending time with our families.

3. Keep your focus on your family, not on your work. As I suggested in chapter 2, a core commitment of every family should be to put family (and faith, as we've just discussed) first. We all know that we should do this, but when our "plate" is as full as the plate of a hungry teenager at an all-you-can-eat buffet, our family often falls by the wayside. I know all too well what a mistake it is not to put family first, as I've described in detail in this chapter. Many times my family commitments were on my "C" list instead of my "A" list, where they belonged. Unfortunately, many parents are headed in the same direction and don't even realize it. So many of the dads and moms who attend my classes tell me that they're unhappy in their jobs, but they feel stuck. When I tell them my story and say that being fired was truly a blessing from God, they give me a hollow look of fright. I tell them that I am not suggesting that they quit their jobs so that they can spend more time at home; I am suggesting that they make finding another job a priority on their "A" list. I am suggesting that they, too, can find a job that makes them feel fulfilled while allowing them to spend more time at home.

Stephen Covey recommends that two-parent families have no more than 1.5 jobs. The .5 reflects a part-time job held by the secondary wage earner. Many couples work out an arrangement where one spouse has a part-time job that allows her or him to be home when the kids are home. If you are the secondary wage earner in your family and your job is unpleasant or stressful, then you need to find a new job! Eventually you'll find that the extra income provides only short-term satisfaction. Likewise, if you're the primary or sole wage earner in your family and your job is unpleasant or stressful, you, too, need to find a new job! In either case, eventually you'll find that the unpleasantness and stress of your job is tearing your family apart.

Believe me, I learned from my mistake. Please, please, please find a job that leaves you time for your family and allows you to be a loving spouse and parent when you are at home. Do whatever it takes to keep your focus on your family.

Parent Point
Finding a More Family-Friendly, Fulfilling Job

1. Identify the kinds of activities that bring joy to your life.

2. Identify what types of jobs would enable you to perform these activities.

3. Identify where these jobs exist and what levels of income may be obtained from these jobs (numerous web sites provide this information).

4. Hire an employment agency or a "head hunter" in order to determine the feasibility of obtaining such a job or jobs. Or, if this is not feasible, talk with someone who has experience in your areas of interest.

5. Work with your family to determine what, if any, changes must be made in order for your family to live on (or be supplemented by) the income of the potential new job. (Remember that many times the actual job you want may require several years of experience that you do not have, requiring you to take a lower-paying job initially.)

6. Adjust your family budget to comply with the new level of income prior to taking the new job. Put the extra money into your savings account.

7. Have the employment agency or headhunter start looking for potential jobs—or begin the process yourself!

4. Let off your "steam." I often use the analogy of a pressure cooker versus a microwave when discussing anger and stress. Just as every pressure cooker must have a release valve that allows the steam to escape, preventing an explosion during the cooking process, so also we must find "release valves" that allow the "steam" in our lives to escape. Unfortunately, most of us tend to be more like a microwave. Although it's a much faster and simpler method of cooking, it doesn't allow the "steam" to escape.

All of us need to "release our steam" at least once a day. For parents, it is especially important to do this before times of "reentry"—times when we are reunited with our children, such as after school or work or any other activity that has separated us. Stephen Covey tells the story of a father who, after driving home from work, would sit in his car in the driveway and ponder this question: "What kind of father and husband do I want to be when I go inside the house?" I have discovered that it takes only ten to fifteen minutes to adequately focus on the person God wants you to be before entering the home.

I wish that I had practiced that exercise myself—especially after my darkest days at work. That's why I now recommend that all working parents adopt a similar practice. At the end of every workday, take about fifteen minutes to prepare yourself for reentry into the home by meditating, praying, reading the Bible, listening to music, or doing something else that helps you to relax. You might choose to do this before leaving work, while driving home—or to school or daycare to pick up the kids—or, like the father in Covey's story, while sitting in the driveway. Single parents, in particular, need this quiet time because they have to perform the duties of both father and mother.

If you're a stay-at-home parent and have been with the kids all day or during the after-school hours, then you get your fifteen minutes after greeting your spouse! Find a place in the house or outside, weather permitting, where you can be alone. Sit in the car or take a walk, if you have to! While you're preparing for reentry, your spouse is spending time with the kids—talking or playing together.

Once you've had your quiet time and have rejoined the family, do some kind of brief activity together before dinner, such as making a salad, setting the table, or helping wash the dirty pots and pans. Now that you are interacting as a family, you are ready to sit down to dinner and share the events of the day—with the television off! Because you've had some quiet time, you will be better prepared to be an effective listener.

I realize that there are many times when various activities will make it impossible for you to have dinner together as a family. However, I hope that you will try to reprioritize some of these activities so that you can have dinner together several times a week. If you begin this custom when the children are young, you have a better chance of continuing the habit as the children get older and their activities increase.

Another great way to "let off steam" is exercise. Many parents take a long walk after the children are in bed. Some exercise in the morning before the kids are awake. Others play sports, either on a team or with friends. When Curt and Beth were young, Carol and I would get a babysitter and play tennis with another couple. Whatever you do, however, remember that if your activities ever compromise your family values in any way, then those activities will begin to generate "steam" instead of release it!

5. Take time for yourself. Though taking time for yourself certainly is a way to let off steam, it's also a way to *prevent* that steam from developing in the first place. Whereas letting off steam is something you do when you're stressed out, taking time for yourself is something that helps you to keep from becoming stressed out! Taking time for yourself each day is absolutely essential to decreasing your overall stress level and controlling your anger.

I am absolutely convinced that both the physical and mental health of the family is only as good as the health of each individual member, beginning with the parents. However, after several years of working with parents, I am also absolutely convinced that the majority of parents, especially moms, put themselves at the bottom of the list. Because moms do tend to give and give and give and put themselves last, I want to address their needs specifically. Although my driving point pertains to all moms, those who are employed outside the home on a full-time basis and those who are not, I want to take a moment to focus on those who have been called "soccer moms," or stay-at-home moms. (Though there are also stay-at-home dads, their number is few in comparison. However, if you happen to be a stay-at-home dad, you, too, may identify with some of what I say.) A lot of these moms attend my classes. Although their children do not always play soccer—sometimes it's baseball or basketball or dance or piano lessons—they tend to believe that they must be present at every one of their children's practices or lessons. They also tend to believe that their children should not ride the school bus. Riding the bus is *punishment* for their children. So they wait in long pickup lines every afternoon. Many of these same moms are also very active in various community organizations. They often tell me that since they don't have full-time jobs (though some do have part-time jobs or jobs that allow them to work out of the home on their own schedules), they feel guilty if they turn down a request to volunteer. Their busy routines also include cooking dinner, helping with homework, and getting the children ready for bed. Of course, moms who have full-time jobs have these same responsibilities and, likewise, never seem to slow down! One mom even told me that, at their house, it's 8:00 P.M. by the time homework begins and 10:00 P.M. before the children are quiet and in their beds. Total exhaustion then sets in, and they all go to sleep.

So, when I tell the parents in my classes that putting family first includes putting themselves first, the moms always give a very loud, sarcastic laugh! One of my biggest failures has been getting busy moms to understand that in order to be physically and mentally fit, they need time for themselves. I suggest several ways they can carve time for themselves out of their busy schedules. First, if they don't want their children riding the bus because they think the bus passengers are a bad influence, they can consider setting up a carpool with other neighbors. (I also recommend that PTOs create carpool sign-up sheets for all school-related activities.) Or, they can do what other communities do and get parent volunteers to ride the buses! (Last year at one of the regional conferences on the family, I met a father who has started a program for dads. In his community, the dads walk the halls in the schools and ride the buses to and from school. Neighborhoods share the load for each bus. He says that most businesses will allow fathers to take time off to ride a bus or walk a hall one day a month.) Second, to free up time in the afternoons and evenings, I recommend they attend only an *occasional* practice to ensure that the coach's or teacher's value system is similar to theirs. Finally, I suggest they create a regular routine for after-school and evening hours, including specific times for free time or play, homework, dinner, family time, and bedtime—incorporating a reasonable rather than excessive number of practices and weekly activities. This not only helps to structure and balance their hectic days but also gives them much-needed "alone time" after the children have gone to bed—on time! Once they find a way to free some time during their busy days and evenings, all moms should use some of this time to do something each day that helps to prevent and relieve stress. Some moms tell me they like to have a facial or a pedicure. Others attend yoga classes or aerobics (some moms exercise during lunch breaks). I have found that therapeutic massage is one of the best-known antidotes for stress. It has been used as a treatment for persons receiving psychological counseling as well as for persons with addictions. Massage can relieve many types of muscle tightness as well as stimulating your nervous system. If you cannot afford a massage, then I recommend parents learn how to give each other a massage! Some moms prefer some kind of activity or hobby they can do with other adults because they enjoy the opportunity to socialize. When Carol was a stay-at-home mom, she looked forward to the times when she got together with other moms. Other moms who have been working all day and caring for their families in the evenings enjoy taking a warm bath or finding a cozy place to read a favorite book. The important thing is not *what* you choose to do but simply that you choose to do *something* that helps you to feel better both physically and mentally.

The fathers who are reading this book may be wondering why I have not discussed the ways they can take time for themselves. If you feel this way, then you are in the minority! I believe that most men do a wonderful job of finding time for themselves, though there are some exceptions (if you're one of the exceptions, then I *urge* you to carve time for yourself out of your busy schedule as well). The gyms are filled with men early in the morning, at lunchtime, and in the early evening. On weekends I see many men playing golf or tennis or attending a sporting event. My hope is to encourage dads to help their wives find time for themselves! After all, the health and welfare of the entire family is at stake!

6. Take a vacation. I have found that vacations can either be stress relievers or stress contributors! Because my company had an "unwritten rule" that employees could not take more than one week of vacation at a time (We were told that if your department could run smoothly for two weeks without you, it could run the additional fifty weeks without you!), our family vacations were always limited to one week. Here's the way a typical vacation would be. We would arrive at our destination on Saturday. By the time we got settled, Saturday was shot. On Sunday, Monday, and Tuesday, we would argue about what activities we wanted to do and where we were going to eat. Usually, I wasn't able to forget about work and truly relax until Wednesday. Finally, on Wednesday, I would be more amiable with my family and more agreeable about where we were going to eat or what activities the children wanted to pursue. Then came Thursday, the day of doom. Thursday was the day when I would realize that we were going back home on Friday. Vacation was almost over, and the things that *I* wanted to do once again didn't happen. My vacation was almost over, and I knew that a lot of catch-up work was waiting for me at the office. Most of the time there also was yard work waiting for me at home. So, I'd be miserable all day, unable to enjoy our last day of "family fun and relaxation."

Books on relaxation suggest that you need two weeks of vacation to really reenergize your batteries. Now that I teach and am able to take two-week vacations in the summertime, I have discovered the truth of this statement. I recommend you make this discovery yourself by extending your next vacation beyond one week. If two weeks are not possible, even a few extra days will give you more time to relax.

Another recommendation is to have one parent—or another adult traveling with you—be the "vacation coordinator." I learned the value of this while on vacation one year with my brother. We were at the beach in South Carolina. My brother, Biff, and his son, Drew, joined my family. On the first full day of vacation, my children started to argue over the activities we would do. I must admit that I was contributing to the argument as well. Finally, my brother offered to be the "vacation coordinator." Each one of us wrote on a piece of paper the number one activity we wanted to do. The only ground rule was that the cost of the activity could not exceed a certain amount to be determined by the adults. Biff's responsibility was to ensure that all seven activities were accomplished prior to the next to last day of vacation. He did a wonderful job. We all returned home happier, and the adults returned home with a lower level of stress. If you will give the vacation coordinator idea a try, I'm confident you will enjoy your vacation much more.

My final recommendation is to take a "minivacation" without the children each year. Each year that we lived in Pittsburgh, my parents would babysit the kids one weekend while Carol and I went away for a minihoneymoon. We never spent a lot of money. We would stay in a motel and swim, play golf, or sightsee. We loved this time, and so did the children and grandparents! When we returned home, everyone in the family was happier. When we left Pittsburgh, we had trouble finding babysitters for weekends. So, whenever my parents would come to see us, we would always spend a night away from home. Whether you can get away for one night or a full weekend, whether you go out of town or stay close to home, this time apart with your spouse will not only help you to reduce your stress but also to nurture your relationship.

It is so important for parents to stay energized. When we are stressed, we are not at our best with each other or with our children. Vacations and weekends away can help us to reduce our stress and relax. Please don't underestimate the importance of relaxation to you and your family!

7. Find a place that allows you to feel close to God. So often we allow the everyday bumps in the road of life to increase our stress. Other times we have a "blowout" in an unseen hole in the road, causing us to feel completely stressed out and alone. Though God is always with us, ready to help, sometimes we forget—and sometimes we even begin to wonder. It happens to each of us.

Not long ago I was in what I call an "emotional recession." My father died a year ago, and we lost Beth's fiancé in a tragic accident. In addition to grieving those losses, I was grieving for thousands of people after the September 11, 2001, tragedy. And so, you might say that I was seeing the world through dirty sunglasses. Whenever I'm in an emotional recession and feeling down, I am disconnected from God. As a result, I tend to place too much importance on nonimportant things. So, one day I "crossed the line" while watching my favorite professional football team. I yelled and screamed at the television as if the outcome of the game would decide my fate in life. Carol later told me that I had not displayed that amount of anger in a long, long time. Luckily, I received help—not from a doctor or therapist, but from the Great Physician. That help came when I found a place where I could feel close to God again.

The holidays were approaching. My mom was going to spend Christmas with my sister, and my brother was going to spend Christmas with his wife's parents. That meant that Carol, Beth, and I would be spending Christmas alone. Our best friends came to our rescue by asking us to join them in Hilton Head, South Carolina. Prior to Curt's death, our family had spent some wonderful vacations at Hilton Head. Now, however, it represented another place full of difficult memories. I was not interested in going, but Carol and Beth were not going to take a no for an answer.

When we first arrived, I was very uptight and not looking forward to the next seven days. My feelings soon changed, however. As always, our friends Dottie and Kelly and their two daughters, Erin and Shannon, treated us as family. On the second day, Carol and I took a wonderful walk on the beach. I have always found water to be very healing. When I am walking beside a lake or an ocean and watching the birds fly across the sky and the fish jump out of the water, I am always reminded that I am one of God's many creatures and am never really alone.

A few days later I road a bike along the coastline. I had been hoping to see a dolphin all week but had come up empty. I decided I wasn't going to leave the beach that day until I saw one. I watched the pelicans dive-bomb the fish. I watched the sea gulls patiently wait for one of the children on the beach to throw them some bread. I saw couples of all ages holding hands. Still, no dolphins. Finally, I came to a sailboat on the beach that was waiting for warmer weather to come. I sat on the boat and watched the coastline like a policeman at a stakeout. All of a sudden, several fins rose out of the water, just outside where the waves were breaking. I was witnessing a large school of dolphins having fun. Eventually, all but one left for deeper water. As I pedaled back up the beach, the one lone dolphin seemed to follow me. When I got back to the entrance to the beach, the dolphin flipped its tail in the air and headed out to sea. As I left the ocean at the end of the week, I once again felt close to God and all of God's creatures.

Once again the ocean had healed my wounds. When I returned home, I felt reenergized to deal with the many bumps that awaited me on my road of life. Once again I was able to view football as just a game men play. Once again I was able to be a better dad for

Beth and a better husband for Carol. Once again I was able to do a better job of handling my negative feelings in a positive way. Most important, once again I realized that I am not traveling down the road of life by myself. God is with me.

God is with each of us. Find a place that allows you to feel close to God—an everyday place as well as a special place—and meet God there. I've learned that if we will only seek God, we will find the help we need.

Handling Your Children's Anger

Now that we've considered some positive ways to release our own anger, let's consider some positive ways we can respond to our children's anger. After all, our children's anger is one of the most frequent negative stimuli we encounter, often generating anger within ourselves. So, how can we learn to handle our children's anger in a positive way? Let me offer six suggestions.

1. Separate yourself from the child's behavior.

Obviously, we cannot suppress our children's anger. So, how do we allow our children to be angry without becoming angry ourselves? As many experts advise, we must learn to separate ourselves from the child's behavior. Whenever possible, the best way to do this is to *physically* separate yourself from the child until the child is able to settle down and discuss his or her feelings calmly. In their book *Parenting with Love and Logic*, Cline and Fay suggest that with time and persistence, parents can train young children to stay in a separate room or area instead of attempting to rejoin their parents. The book includes some wonderful, practical suggestions tied to specific situational scenarios, including examples using older children. Even older children and teens need to know that you will not be the victim of their anger but will be happy to discuss their feelings with them calmly as soon as they're able. Once the child has calmed down, then you are ready to implement suggestion 2.

2. Listen to your child when he or she is angry.

Usually, as few as ten to fifteen minutes of separation will allow a younger child to regain control. Older children and teens may want more time alone. Once the child has calmed down and is ready to talk, sit down together and discuss why the child is upset. Be sure to say that whenever your child does not talk to you with proper respect, you will not listen to what he or she has to say. If the child's behavior gets out of control again, separate yourself from the child and try again later. As you talk together, incorporate suggestion 3 as appropriate, which is modeling the "I feel" process.

3. Model the "I feel" process.

Another integral part of teaching children how to control their negative feelings is to model for them the "I feel" process. One of the most effective times to model this process is when your child has made you angry. As you talk with your child at those times, follow these simple steps.

Step 1. State *how* you feel.
Step 2. State *when* you have these feelings.
Step 3. State *why* you have these feelings.
Step 4. Tell your child *what* you want.

Let's say, for example, that your child has missed curfew. How would you feel? You might feel angry, disappointed, worried, or some combination of the three. Begin by telling your child *how* you feel. The *when* of step 2 always begins the same way: "I feel this way when you don't respect our family rules." The second part of the statement, however, varies according to the specific family rule that has been broken. So, in the case of a missed curfew, you would say, "I feel this way when you don't respect our family rules by missing your curfew." Next, clarify *why* you feel the way you do as you emphasize the value of the particular rule your child has broken. For example, you might say something along these lines: "Safety is an important family value, and that's why we've given you a curfew. I/We shouldn't have to be worrying about where you

167

are." Finally, tell your child *what* you want to happen. For example, you might say, "I expect you to respect our family rules, including your curfew, and the consequence for missing your curfew is a new curfew. From now on, your curfew will be. . . ."

The purpose of modeling "I feel" statements in this way is to teach your children to express their own feelings with words. When we model this process consistently, eventually our children will learn it as well. Using "I feel" statements not only teaches our children, but it also helps us remain in control of our emotions.

4. Teach the six-step problem solving method.

Another useful "tool" is the six-step problem solving method (adapted and modified from the resource *Facts, Feelings, Family, and Friends*). There is a direct link between frustration and anger. Many times children become angry because they don't have the necessary tools or skills to complete a task or solve a problem. No doubt you've observed this firsthand. Your happy toddler suddenly falls into a screaming, kicking fit because he can't get a zipper zipped or a button buttoned. Or your fourth grader who has been quietly doing her homework suddenly throws her books on the floor in anger when she doesn't understand an assignment. Or your teenager stomps across the floor and slams the door to his room because he got a poor test score or had a bad afternoon at practice. Sound familiar?

When I was starting my teaching ministry, a private Christian elementary school asked me to help them develop a life skills training program that would teach the students how to cope with the many problems they would be facing in the coming years. They recognized that those children who learn the life skixlls they need are much happier than those who don't. One of the most important life skills we can teach our children is problem solving. Children who don't know how to solve problems are unable to make difficult decisions, and children who are unable to make difficult decisions grow up to be adults who are unable to make difficult decisions.

One of the greatest advantages you can give your children is to teach them how to solve problems. So, whenever they have a problem to solve, walk them through the six-step problem solving method. Before you know it, they'll be walking themselves through it automatically. Here it is:

Six-Step Problem Solving Method

1. Ask your child to state the problem in his or her words.
2. Ask your child how this problem makes him or her feel.
3. a) Have your child tell you the various choices he or she has for solving the problem.
   b) You make your suggestion.
4. a) Have your child identify the consequences of each choice.
   b) You identify the consequence of your suggestion.
5. Consider what resources are available to help solve the problem.
6. Decide what choice is best (morally right), and do it.

Let's consider each step in more detail.

1. Ask your child to state the problem in his or her words. When your child comes to you with a problem, remain quiet while you listen to what your child has to say. Many times I would make the mistake of immediately taking ownership of my children's problems. Sometimes you will need to ask a few questions to help confirm your understanding of their problem.

2. Ask your child how this problem makes him or her feel. This step is the one most parents forget, yet it is extremely important. You will gain more in-depth understanding of your child's point of view when you understand his or her feelings. For example, jealousy is a far different problem than anger. Feeling alone is a far different problem to solve than feeling sad. Again, when I was at my worst as a parent, I didn't really care about how my children felt. I only cared about how the problem made *me* feel. When working with elementary school students today, I am always amazed at the number of feeling words they know how to use. Most children are more in tune with their feelings than we may think.

3. Have your child tell you the various choices he or she has for solving the problem. Actually, this step should be divided into two parts. Part one is the child's input, and part two is your input. Your knowledge base should allow for a few more choices. It's important, however, that you intentionally place value on your child's choices and refrain from criticizing or judging your child's

169

input. Remember that the next step will give you the opportunity to critique each choice. Remember, also, to welcome any "off the wall" choices or choices your child states just to make you laugh. Finally, there may be occasions when your child cannot think of any choice. When this happens, help your child brainstorm ideas without dominating the conversation. Try saying something such as, "Beth, what do you think of this idea?"

4. Identify the consequences of each choice. I recommend you divide this step into two parts as well. First, the child states the consequences, and then you can add your input. Again, it is important to maintain impartiality. I will never forget the first time I taught the six-step process to a third grade class. I asked them to tell what they should do if they were home by themselves and a stranger came to the door. One of the boys said, "Mr. Williams, I would go upstairs and get my father's gun." When we got to step 4, I asked the same boy to tell me the consequences of his choice. He said that the man would leave the house. When I asked his classmates for their opinions, many stated that the child might get hurt or killed if he had the gun. I also put in my two cents' worth! This step enabled us to show the dangers of his suggested "solution."

5. Consider what resources are available to help solve the problem. This step is intended to help children think of adults other than their parents who might be able to help them solve a particular problem. When we are not around and our children have problems to solve, we want them to think of other adults who could offer knowledge or wisdom or help—perhaps a teacher, a coach, a minister, a youth pastor, an aunt or uncle, a grandparent, or a neighbor. Again, a good way to help children understand this step is to ask them who they might call if they were home alone and needed help. Or you might set up another scenario: "You and your younger brother or sister are home alone after school. You need to get to practice, and your younger brother or sister wants to stay home alone. You know he or she is too young to stay home alone, so you tell the child that he or she has to go to practice with you. The child becomes upset. What do you do?"

At the Christian elementary school where I teach the six-step problem solving method, I am able to add another dimension to this step by asking the children to consider another resource always available to them: God. Each time I teach the method, I suggest they begin the practice of asking themselves this question whenever faced with a problem or a choice: "What would Jesus want me to do?" It is this question alone, I explain, that enables us to make the right—or the moral—choice. This leads us to the final step.

6. Decide what choice is best (morally right), and do it. Sadly, it seems that so many youth and adults in our society today have lost the ability to make moral decisions. Instead of choosing to do what is right, they choose to do what feels good. So much of the "Parenting on Point" philosophy resides on this issue. If you accept the Golden Rule as a core value for your family and practice it on a daily basis, your children will learn to make the right choices, the moral choices, and feel good about them as well. Leading our families along God's path means making moral choices.

When we follow the six-step problem solving method, we do not take ownership of the problem. In other words, the child should feel that he or she has developed the answer, rather than us. Remaining calm is essential to the process, for this allows us to proceed orderly from one step to the next. If we become angry, we can easily move from step 1 to step 6 and skip all the others! "You (the child) will take this action because I (the parent) told you to take this action!" So many parents who now follow these six steps tell me that the process itself helps them to remain calm because it's a structured approach to solving unstructured problems. Best of all, parents tell me that by using the six-step method, they spend more time communicating with their children. Thus, we have another win/win idea for you to try!

It's Up to You

When Curt died and I questioned why God didn't save him, my minister responded, "God gives every person free will, the power to choose." I had to learn to accept that, on that tragic day, a man chose to drink and drive. Likewise, all the people in the bar chose not to take his car keys away. Each of us has an independent will to choose whether we will act like animals, expressing our negative feelings in negative ways, or be the moral and loving human beings that God wants us to be, releasing our anger in positive ways. The choice is yours. It's up to you.

Please, please, please don't underestimate the damage that rage can cause in your life and the life of your family. If you're still having trouble handling your anger after trying the suggestions in this chapter, please seek professional help. My life is better today because I sought professional help. I truly believe—and many, many others agree with me—that seeking help is the evidence of strength, not weakness.

QUESTIONS TO PONDER

1. What are the keys issues or situations that make you angry? What steps can you take to eliminate or resolve one or more of these issues or situations?

2. Do you know when you "cross the line" with others? How does this make you feel?

3. Are you able to ask for forgiveness when you have "crossed the line"? If not, why?

4. Do you have a "pause button" or other methods for releasing your anger in a more positive way?

5. Do you find structured approaches such as using "I feel" statements and the six-step problem solving method helpful? If not, what can you do to improve your communications skills when angry?

6. Do you have a soul mate? Does each of your children have one?

7. What place(s) allow you to feel close to God?

10

NURTURING YOUR CHILD—
AND YOURSELF

Scripture Link

But I don't need to write to you about the Christian love that should be shown among God's people. For God himself has taught you to love one another.
—1 Thessalonians 4:9 NLT

May you experience the love of Christ, though it is so great you will never fully understand it. Then you will be filled with the fullness of life and power that comes from God. *—Ephesians 3:19 NLT*

Even to your old age and gray hairs
I am he, I am he who will sustain you.
I have made you and I will carry you;
I will sustain you and I will rescue you.
—Isaiah 46:4 NIV

Most dictionaries define *nurturing* using words such as supporting, sustaining, educating, training, disciplining, instructing, and schooling. Another good synonym is cherishing. My work with children has confirmed to me that children need nurturing on a daily basis. Contrary to the belief of many parents, the amount of nurturing our children need does not decrease as they get older; it actually increases. In fact, after completing my fifty-fourth year on this earth, I am convinced that we adults need daily nurturing just as much as our children do.

Nurturing is the cement that holds the foundation of our self-worth together. It is also the "tool" that repairs the foundation when cracks result from times of "unsettling."

For both children and adults, nurturing is integrally related to our capacity to feel God's love for us. When we're children, nurturing allows us to know and feel God's love. When we're adults, nurturing breaks down the many barriers we continually create that make us feel separated from God's love. As human beings, we all receive nurturing from many different sources—parents, siblings, children, other relatives, friends, teachers, coaches, soul mates, and on and on. Likewise, as human beings, we all nurture others. I believe that we adults have a *responsibility* to nurture others—not only our own children, but also the many other children and adults we encounter on a daily basis. I feel very strongly about our responsibility to children, in particular—those in our neighborhoods, our schools, and our churches. Most churches see this responsibility as a calling from God—a calling that begins when a child is baptized or dedicated and the members of the congregation agree to be responsible for the child's spiritual development.

In this chapter we will explore some of the ways that we can fulfill our responsibility to nurture others—as well as satisfy our own need for nurturing. Let's begin by discussing ways we can nurture our children.

Fill Your Children's "Buckets" with Scoops of Love

Experts agree that our children have a need to receive positive reinforcement, words of praise, acts of kindness, and sometimes forgiveness on a daily basis. They say that when children feel secure in their surroundings and cherished by us, their loved ones, they are more receptive to our guidance. Though the metaphors the experts use are different, the general concept is the same. In his book *The 7 Habits of Highly Effective Families,* Stephen Covey uses the image of a child's emotional "bank account," which must be filled with certain deposits made by the adults in the child's life. Similarly, in their book *The Five Love Languages of Children,* Gary Chapman and Ross Campbell talk about the many ways we adults can fill a child's emotional "tank." I like to use the analogy of a "bucket" because I like the clear mental image of filling a child's bucket with "scoops of love." We all can remember happily playing in a sandbox or at the beach, scooping sand into a bucket until it's full and then carefully turning it over to make the perfect sandcastle. In a sense, that's the way we should approach the task of parenting. To nurture our children—to ensure that our children feel God's love and become the loving persons God created them to be—we must fill their buckets with scoops of love on a daily basis.

The Scriptures give us specific guidance for how to nurture our children, telling us to be kind and good to our children (as God is good to us), to forgive them and seek their forgiveness (as God so graciously forgives us), to be trustworthy (as God is always trustworthy), and to teach them integrity (as God teaches us to be persons of integrity). Using Scripture as our foundational springboard, let's consider these important "scoops of love" we need to fill our children's buckets with each and every day.

1. A scoopful of kindness

Scripture Link
*As God's chosen ones, holy
and beloved, clothe yourselves with compassion, kindness, humility, meekness, and patience.*
—Colossians 3:12

Don't make your children angry by the way you treat them.   *—Ephesians 6:4b NLT*

Do to others as you would have them do to you.
—Luke 6:31

The Golden Rule: Most of us teach it to our children, but do we practice it ourselves? Our children not only need to hear our kind words, but they also need to see our kind actions. When I do presentations on bullying behavior, I ask students to tell me the last time someone in their class demonstrated a simple gesture of kindness. Only a few hands go up. In contrast, when I ask if they ever get their feelings hurt at home, many hands go up! Their response confirms that kindness is lacking not only in our schools, but also in our homes. Whenever I discuss the "scoop of kindness" in my parenting classes, I always see guilt in many parents' eyes. Home is the last opportunity a child has each day for receiving a scoopful of kindness, and, unfortunately, it's often a missed opportunity.

At work, I was known as a very caring boss, but at home I took on a different persona. What made this even more alarming was that I could be kind to my children's friends, but not to my own children. If I had children to raise today, I would ask myself every night before going to sleep: "How many scoops of kindness did I put into each child's bucket today?" It's a question each of us should ask.

PARENT POINT
Everyday Acts of Kindness

1. Give each of your children a big hug and kiss before they leave for school (or, with preschoolers, first thing in the morning).

2. Put at least one of their favorite foods in their lunchboxes each day.

3. Be an effective listener when they talk to you.

4. Spend that extra ten minutes helping them with a homework assignment.

5. Agree to watch "their" show instead of yours.

6. Help them with a chore when their other responsibilities become overwhelming.

7. Praise the good grades or efforts more than you criticize the bad grades.

8. Be angry at the behavior, not the child.

---

2. A scoopful of grace

Scripture Link

Bear with one another and, if anyone has a complaint against another, forgive each other; just as the Lord has forgiven you, so you also must forgive.
—Colossians 3:13

So when you are offering your gift at the altar, if you remember that your brother or sister [or child] has something against you, leave your gift there before the altar and go; first be reconciled to your brother or sister, and then come and offer your gift.
—Matthew 5:23-24

For me, grace and forgiveness are synonymous. Because God has shown us grace by forgiving our sins, we also must forgive our children when they do wrong. Though at times we may think it's unnecessary to say it, our children need to hear those three simple words: "I forgive you." These words begin the healing process between parent and child. However, our words are not enough. We then must demonstrate forgiveness through our actions. If our actions continue to express our disappointment rather than our forgiveness, then our words become meaningless. Our words and actions must work together in order to cement the bond of trust.

Expressing our forgiveness, however, can be difficult. Parents often ask me if they should forgive their children when they do not apologize and ask for forgiveness. The answer is "Yes!" When people ask how I was able to forgive the man who killed Curt since he never said he was sorry or asked for forgiveness, I tell them that forgiveness is not only for the person who has done something wrong. Forgiveness is also for the one who has been wronged. You see, I forgave the drunk driver for my sake, not for his. I forgave him in order to release my anger and prevent it from turning to rage, which I knew would eventually destroy me. I chose to forgive him at Curt's funeral in front of the hundreds of young people who were there because I wanted those young people to go home remembering Curt with love in their hearts, not anger or rage. And finally, I forgave the driver because I knew in my heart that God wanted me to.

Likewise, expressing forgiveness to our children, even when they haven't asked for it, helps us to release our anger as we put a heaping scoopful of grace into our children's buckets.

Another important aspect of grace is telling our children that we're sorry when we're the ones who have done wrong. Unfortunately, so many children tell me that they are always the ones apologizing at home—never their parents. When we do not model the behavior of apologizing for our children at home, they do not practice this behavior away from home. My work with students confirms this; I've discovered that very few students apologize to others. However, I continue to be amazed by their responses when I give them the opportunity to apologize to one another during my workshop on bullying behavior. As they role-play the bully, the victim, and the bystander, and we talk together about what it feels like to be bullied, I have the boys and girls come to the front of the room and apologize for the hurtful things they've said and done to one another, as well as for not standing up for the victims. Sometimes a student will even find the courage to apologize to a specific boy or girl. Then, they have the opportunity to offer one another forgiveness. Most do—often with tears in their eyes. I always feel God's presence in the room when we do this exercise.

I share this with you to emphasize the importance of modeling the process of apologizing in our homes. Failing to set the correct example for our children not only prevents them from learning to apologize; it also makes them lose their trust in us. They begin to believe that there is a double standard in the world. They have to act one way while adults can act another way. If we are going to help our children stay on point, we must "talk the talk" *and* "walk the walk" when it comes to apologizing.

Parents often ask me why I think it's so hard for us to apologize to our children. Obviously, most of us don't like to admit that we've done something wrong, particularly if our wrongdoing has hurt the feelings of someone we love. Yet we actually hurt our children even more by refusing to apologize. When we hurt our children's feelings in some way, they *need* to hear us say, "I am sorry."

These words are also part of the glue that cements the bond of trust between parent and child.

Many times as a father, I knew that I had made a bad decision, but I was too proud to apologize. It was too humbling. So often we feel that way because we're worried that the image we have tried to create will be tarnished or destroyed if we apologize to our children. This image protects us from allowing our children to know that we are fallible. The truth is, our children need to know that we all make mistakes and that God does not expect us to be perfect. They also need to know that God does, however, expect us to apologize and ask for forgiveness. As I discovered after learning to control my anger and keep God in the center of my life, it is easier to apologize when we remind ourselves that this is what God wants and expects us to do. And because apologizing is truly a Godlike behavior, it actually makes us feel good inside!

As parents, our goal should be to apologize as soon as we realize our mistake. Sometimes, however, this realization doesn't occur until after we have calmed down and regained control of our emotions. Whenever the realization occurs, we should apologize immediately. If the child is away from home for the time being or is asleep, then we should apologize at the very next opportunity. How we apologize is just as important as when. Here is a four-step process to both model and teach your children to apologize:

PARENT POINT
The Art of Apologizing

1. Say that you are sorry.
2. Tell *why* you are sorry.
3. Tell what you will do differently in the future—how you will change your behavior.
4. Ask for forgiveness—from the other person and, privately, from God.

We all have our bad days, and when we are out of sorts and hurt our children, whether intentionally or unintentionally, we need to apologize and ask for their forgiveness—again, before they go to bed if at all possible. When we apologize, we not only model an important behavior we want our children to learn, but we also put a scoopful of grace into their buckets.

3. A scoopful of trust

Scripture Link

It is impossible for God to lie. Therefore, we who have fled to him for refuge can take new courage, for we can hold on to his promise with confidence. This confidence is like a strong and trustworthy anchor for our souls. —Hebrews 6:18-19a NLT

Keep all the promises you make. . . . It is better to say nothing than to promise something that you don't follow through on. —Ecclesiastes 5:4b-5 NLT

One of the most important ways we earn our children's trust is by keeping our promises. When we keep our promises, our children feel loved and cared for. For younger children, promises are not only promises but also covenants, sacred trusts. Promises are extremely important to older children as well, though some experts claim that older children are slightly more adept at handling a broken promise. So many students have told me that their feelings are hurt when their parents break a promise. When this happens, they begin to lose their trust in all promises. They see them broken too often, including a promise that is broken by approximately 50 percent of their parents—a promise broken by divorce.

As parents, we need to be more careful about saying the words, "I promise." We need to use words such as "I'll try to be there," or "I'll do my best to make the game." And if we fail to make the game, we should apologize and ask for forgiveness because the hurt the child feels is still formidable. I am not suggesting for one minute, however, that we should never say "I promise." Making and keeping promises is crucial to the parent-child relationship. As

I've said, we demonstrate our trustworthiness to our children when we keep our promises. Each time we make and keep a promise—whether it's to be at our children's recitals and games or to always love them—we're putting a scoopful of trust into their buckets.

4. A scoopful of integrity

> ### Scripture Link
>
> *I will lead a life of integrity in my own home.*
> —*Psalm 101:2c NLT*
>
> *In your teaching show integrity, seriousness and soundness of speech that cannot be condemned, so that those who oppose you may be ashamed because they have nothing bad to say about us.*   —*Titus 2:7b-8 NIV*

If we want to teach our children to have integrity, then we must demonstrate integrity ourselves. One of the most effective ways to do this is to refrain from gossiping and talking negatively about others. As I learned in an educational course on the behavior of bullies, gossiping and saying negative things about others are actually acts of violence—verbal violence. If this sounds harsh to you, consider the effect negative speech has on our children. Experts agree that when our children hear us talk negatively about other people, they think we must talk negatively about them, too, when they are not around. Likewise, when our children hear us talking negatively about their role models—the important adults in their lives—they feel as if we are actually talking negatively about them. Why? Children identify themselves with the adults they admire and respect. It's as if those adults are holding mirrors in front of themselves so that when admiring children look at them, the children see themselves as reflections of those adults. Therefore, when our children hear us criticize these adults, they consider us to be criticizing them as well.

Therefore, if we want to build trust with our children, we must be more careful about what we say about others. There truly is some merit to the old expression, "If you don't have anything nice to say about someone, don't say anything at all." Remember, our children model us, and we must set the right example.

I challenge you, as I challenge all the parents who attend my classes, to try not to say anything unkind about someone for an entire week. Parents tell me that, in addition to having a very quiet house, this exercise makes them realize how often they say negative things about other people.

Here's another exercise I'd like you to try. Write down on a piece of paper the names of the individuals you tend to openly criticize (both adults and children/youth), and ask yourself why you criticize these people so much. Ask yourself if any of these individuals is important in your children's lives. Make an effort on a daily basis not to say critical things about these people in front of your children. On those occasions when you slip up and allow criticism to slip out, apologize to your children. Say, "I'm sorry for criticizing your friend/that person. That was wrong. Please forgive me."

If you will become more sensitive to and careful in what you say about others, you will not only set a good example for your children but also will put a scoopful of integrity into their buckets.

Try Not to Empty Your Children's Buckets!

Just as there are various ways to fill our children's buckets with love, so also there are various ways to empty them. Obviously, if we don't perform acts of kindness, if we are unforgiving, if we never say that we are sorry, if we prove untrustworthy, and if we gossip or say negative things about others, we are emptying our children's buckets. We also empty their buckets when we are too critical of them or when we complain too much about their behavior. Perhaps the worst way we can empty our children's buckets is when we allow our anger to become rage, striking out either verbally or, in some cases, physically. All of these hurtful acts deplete the love from our children's buckets, eventually leaving them empty.

I wish there were a way to literally count the scoops of love in a child's bucket. If we could, then we might occasionally rationalize that the hurtful thing we just did wasn't so bad because the bucket still has plenty of love! Actually, there is a way we can monitor the love in our children's buckets, and we should do it each and every day. Perhaps a story will help to illustrate.

Some time ago I bought one of those meters that you apply on the outside of a propane tank. As the propane is used, the meter acts like a gauge and tells how much gas is still inside. One day as I was beginning to grill something, the tank ran out of gas. I picked up the tank, and it was as light as a feather. "Duh! An empty tank!" Obviously, the meter wasn't working. The next day, after filling the tank, I purchased and filled a second tank so that I would never run out of propane gas while grilling again!

Keeping track of the love in a child's bucket is a similar process. Instead of relying on a meter to tell us that the bucket is full, we need to "pick up the child" and decide for ourselves. In other words, we must spend time with the child and talk with the child in order to determine how the child is feeling. Likewise, the idea of buying a second tank is analogous to being sure we put scoops of love into the child's bucket each day, rather than emptying it. Since we don't know how much love has been removed during the day, we must talk to the child in order to gauge the level of love for ourselves. Remember that our children's buckets can be emptied during school and other activities that we are not personally monitoring. In addition to talking with your child, watch his or her body language for clues. Recall the child's behavior since being at home. Has the child seemed moody or easily agitated? Has the child had an argument with his or her siblings?

No child feels loved—by you or even by God—when his or her bucket is empty. I believe that when children are young, their image of God comes from their relationships with parents and other caring adults. For children, love is a verb, and our actions—as well as those of other caring adults in their lives—make them feel loved. Each night before you go to bed, then, ask yourself this important question: "What is the level of love in my child's bucket today?" If you feel that your child's bucket is low or perhaps empty, go to the child before he or she goes to sleep and express how much you love your child and how special the child is to you. Take the child a cookie and a glass of milk. If you, personally, have removed a few scoops that day, apologize and ask your child for forgiveness. Children are very forgiving, and a little bit of love and caring can fill a bucket very quickly. No one, especially God, expects us to be perfect; but I do believe that God expects us to do our best to keep our children's buckets full.

Watch for Children Who Have "Holes" in Their Buckets, and Do What You Can to Repair Them

Unfortunately, some children not only have empty buckets; they also have *holes* in their buckets. Holes appear in a child's bucket when it has been empty for a long time. I have discovered that many of the bullies and/or their victims in the classroom have holes in their buckets. I also have observed that the majority of children in the juvenile court system and summer school programs where I work have buckets with holes. Whenever I speak to these children, my verbal scoops simply drain through the holes. I've found that the first thing I must do, then, is to repair their buckets. I have found that only one thing repairs their buckets: trust. I must earn their trust.

Ideally, the parents and/or other adults in the children's lives who have broken their trust and created the holes in their buckets should be the ones to repair those holes. Unfortunately, this doesn't always happen. Therefore, as a caring adult, I can repair their buckets by helping them to trust adults once again. When I talk to these troubled young people, I tell them my story and the pain that I've felt since Curt died. I then tell them that I am able to carry this pain and move forward if I know that my words have had a positive impact on their lives. I tell them that I love them and that they are very special to me. They believe me. The counselors and teachers who work with these young people tell me that many of them start making positive changes in their lives. I know that, alone, I'm not that powerful; but God is. And with God's help, I can repair their buckets. With God's help, every caring adult can do the same.

Over a period of time, a child's trust can be regained when one or more caring adults maintain a nurturing relationship with the child. Once this trust is regained and the child's bucket is repaired, then any scoop of love put into that child's bucket will remain in the bucket and not drain through. If a child's bucket is never repaired—if no caring adults earn the child's trust and make deposits into the child's bucket—then the child is put "at risk." The child is "at risk" to never return to God's path. When I talk to these at-risk young people, I feel their anger toward their world. Many of them have become violent.

184

Through all the research I have done on the subject, I've learned that there are some common threads among at-risk children.

1. At-risk children keep their feelings inside.

Without an effective relationship with a caring adult, one who is a good listener and who knows how to express his or her feelings, a child does not learn how to express his or her own feelings. Sometimes a child learns how to express feelings but stops doing so after his or her feelings are rejected or ignored. I've witnessed children hiding their feelings time and time again. As I continue to work with thousands of children each year, I'm continually amazed and disappointed by the number of children who keep their feelings in a jar—a jar whose lid is screwed on tight and is buried deep underground! You see, when we adults fail to build trust with the children in our lives—which involves putting scoops of love into their buckets and helping them feel God's love—they learn to hide their feelings instead of expressing them. Eventually, however, all of these hidden feelings will come out of the jar, usually in some kind of "explosion." As we have seen in years past with episodes such as the Columbine tragedy, suppressed feelings can even generate horrific acts of violence. The building of trust with young people helps children learn how to express their feelings in a positive way and is paramount in keeping children on point.

2. At-risk children have no one at "home."

When I first heard of this "common thread" among at-risk children, I thought the experts meant that no parent or guardian was at home in the physical sense. With the increasing number of families with two working parents, this made sense to me. However, I was wrong. What this means is that even when parents or guardians are at home physically, they are not at home mentally. In other words, they are stressed out—by their jobs and by the many other demands and responsibilities of life.

Once again we see the importance of alleviating the stress in our lives! I've said it before and I'll say it again: Please find a job that allows you to be the loving parent and spouse God wants you to be; a job that allows you to be the person your family needs you to be; a job that allows you always to be "at home" mentally.

3. At-risk children have usually been bullied or excluded.

A third and final "common thread" among at-risk children is that they have been—or currently are being—bullied or rejected in some way by others. "Bullying" happens when someone with more power unfairly hurts someone with less power over and over again. Both boys and girls can be bullies. Power may be physical strength, social skill, verbal ability, or another resource. I have learned that there are eighteen acts of violence that bullies can use. The nonphysical acts include eye rolling, gossiping, gesturing, staring/leering, stalking, writing graffiti, threatening, name calling, ridiculing, and intimidation. Other acts of violence include stealing, damaging property, sexual harassment, spitting/pushing, shoving/punching, hitting/kicking, flashing a weapon, stabbing someone, and shooting someone with a gun.

Through my conversations with children, I have found that social acts of violence are the most damaging. As we all know, feeling excluded from the group can be so painful. When I ask students what they can do to keep fellow students from feeling excluded, they suggest things such as calling them by their first names, sitting with them in the cafeteria, asking them to play with them/their group at recess, and asking them to come over to their houses. As parents, we can encourage our children to take these brave steps. Sometimes it requires them to learn the difficult lesson that reaching out to those who have been rejected or excluded often results in their own rejection or exclusion from the clique. When that happens, we can let them know how proud we are of them for taking a stand and reaching out to children who are mistreated at school.

Unfortunately, cliques are not limited to our schools. Whenever I speak to church youth groups about social exclusion, I'm continually amazed at the number of parents who either "have their heads in the sand" or simply live in a world of denial, thinking that all children in the youth group are accepted as part of the group. After talking with the youth and their directors, I always talk with the parents. I remind them that it is every adult's responsibility to make sure that all children feel God's love, which is something that cannot happen if there are cliques within the youth group—or on the team or in the drama club or in the neighborhood. I also remind them that research indicates nonphysical violence such as bullying and excluding others ruins lives and sometimes leads to physical violence. The good news is that there's something we can do about it.

For starters, we need to be more sensitive to the bullying behavior and the many nonphysical acts of violence that occur daily in our schools, churches, and other youth organizations. As your awareness increases, ask yourself how *you* will respond.

Help Your Children Say "Yes" to Three Key Questions

In her book *Our Last Best Shot*, Laura Sessions Stepp confirms that in order to feel accepted, children in early adolescence need to be able to say yes to three key questions. Although this book is intended to help the reader understand children between the ages of ten and fourteen, I have found many of her points to be applicable to all children (and even adults). Here I offer my reflections on each of these questions and its relevance to all children's well-being and self-esteem.

1. "Am I loved? Am I loving?"

We are created in the image of a loving God. We are created to love God, who loves us, and to love others. However, as Laura Sessions Stepp points out in her book, it is very difficult to be loving unless you feel loved yourself. As I have stated previously, I firmly believe that children do not feel God's love unless they feel loved by others, beginning with their parents and their siblings. So, the first and most important way we can help our children answer yes to this important two-part question is to love them unconditionally. How? By loving our children even when they disappoint us; by separating the behavior from the child and directing our anger at the behavior, not the child; by forgiving them when they are wrong and apologizing when we are wrong; by filling their buckets with scoops of love every day; by being effective listeners and trying to see things through their eyes; by spending more time with them and supporting their gifts and talents; and by setting limits and boundaries and consistently enforcing effective consequences. In short, by keeping them on point—on the path that God wants us to follow.

In *The Five Love Languages of Children,* which I referenced earlier in the chapter, Gary Chapman and Ross Campbell suggest that the best way to express love to a child (and, consequently, to fill the child's emotional "tank" or "bucket") is to speak the child's "love language." They explain that a love language is one of several ways that children express and respond to love. I'd like to highlight the three primary love languages: (1) physical touch, (2) words of affirmation, and (3) quality time.

First, children whose primary love language is physical touch need lots of hugs and kisses, pats on the back or on the head, and physical play. When they're younger, lap time while reading or watching TV is important; as they get older, playing sports together can be an effective substitute. Second, children whose primary love language is words of affirmation need to constantly hear words of affection, endearment, praise, encouragement, and positive guidance. These children are also very sensitive to our tone of voice, particularly when we are correcting their behavior. Finally, children whose primary love language is quality time need us to give them their undivided attention when we're communicating with them. In fact, their need for our attention is so great that they often will exhibit *bad* behavior in order to get it! These children need quality time with each parent on a one-on-one basis as well as in a family setting, such as at the dinner table. So, if you want to show your children unconditional love, pay attention to their love languages and adapt your expressions of love accordingly.

In addition to loving our children unconditionally, we can help them to feel loved and loving by surrounding them with other loving people. I share the belief that it takes a community to raise a child, and I believe that it is much easier for a child to feel truly loved and be truly loving if that child feels he or she is loved by the community. Actually, there are various "subcommunities" in every child's life, including relatives, friends, neighbors, schools, and so forth. I believe, however, that one of the most important and influential communities in a child's life is the community of faith.

A "church family" has always played an important role in the life of my family. When we lived in Pittsburgh and were active in our church there, our children always felt loved by many people. Then, when we moved away, we struggled to find another church family where we felt we belonged. Eventually, after moving again, this time to Nashville, we were able to find a church home that filled the void. As we all became active in various church activities, we began to feel more and more loved and supported by our church family.

This church had a wonderful youth choir whose director would allow any teenager to join. The highlight of the choir experience was the summer tour. Because of Curt's commitment to tennis, which involved summer tennis tournaments, he was unable to go on the tour; so, for three years, he refused to join the youth choir. Then, after receiving a tennis scholarship his senior year of high school, Curt finally had a free summer and was able to join the choir. While on tour that summer, they sang at hospitals, retirement homes, and shelters. Each morning they received Holy Communion together. On the last morning, each choir member served another member the bread and juice. Beth was the one to serve Curt. Afterward, he broke down and cried. The love he felt from the group was overwhelming. All the choir members surrounded Curt and gave him a group hug. Later, when he told me about that meaningful moment, he said, "I was so embarrassed, Dad." I told him not to worry because I always cry when I feel the love of Christ.

There's no better way to help our children feel loved and loving than to introduce them to the love of Christ. Find a community of faith where you feel at home and stay active in the life of that community.

2. *"Am I competent?"*

A child needs to be able to say that he or she is competent at something. As parents, our duty is to help our children find their "thing"—something they're good at doing; something they enjoy. As I've mentioned, however, the problem is that we tend to follow society's lead and turn instantly to sports—whether we have boys or girls. If you don't believe it, try this test. First, talk with the staff of the various high schools in your community in order to determine the total percentage of high school students who are active in sports. In the area where I live and work, we have estimated the percentage to be between 10 and 15 percent. Then go to the elementary schools and do the same thing. This time the figure should be well over 50 percent!

As a parent, I was no exception. I've already confessed that I, too, fell into the trap of pushing Beth into sports. Basically she didn't like sports—well, let's say not as much as I wanted her to! Carol came to the rescue by ignoring my efforts to make our daughter an athlete and encouraging Beth to become active in the arts. Beth attended an elementary school that required all fifth grade students to play the violin. After playing the violin for a year, she began learning to play the clarinet. Somewhere along the way, she took some piano lessons. Carol also enrolled Beth in a dance class. I vividly remember going to a talent show at Beth's school and watching her dance to a Beach Boy's tune. Every time I hear this tune today I think of Beth dancing on that stage. She was clearly the most natural and talented dancer on stage throughout the entire talent show. When she "kicked it up a bit," the audience went crazy—especially the boys in her class! There was no doubt in my mind that she had discovered the special gift that God had given her.

We parents can help our children find an activity that makes them feel competent if we follow several important rules. (1) We should not allow our own life experiences to cloud our vision. (2) We must remember that competency does not mean excellency. A child can feel competent at an activity without being excellent at the activity. (3) We need to be patient. (4) We need to be supportive while providing some discipline. (5) Finally, for some of our children, disappointments will precede competency. When this happens, we must help our children deal with these disappointments.

When Beth entered high school, she decided that she wanted to try out for the football/basketball cheerleading squad. She thought that she had performed well during the tryouts, but she didn't make the team because she lacked the necessary gymnastic skills. She was very disappointed. Because we had always encouraged Beth to keep trying and because she had a high level of self-esteem, she tried out for the wrestling team's cheerleading squad. Gymnastics wasn't supposed to be as important for this squad. This time many of the older members on the squad told Beth that she did very well during the tryouts and she should make the team.

She didn't. The second disappointment was harder for her to handle than the first one. During our many discussions with Beth, we discovered that what she really wanted was simply to be involved in an activity at school. There was no way for her to utilize her love for dancing in the school.

The following year, Carol and Beth noticed that the popularity of high school dance teams was growing. So they found a teacher to be the sponsor, and down the road they went! Initially, the school was less than enthusiastic because the old guard still considered cheerleaders to be the major source of entertainment at sporting events. However, when the team was allowed to perform, they brought the house down. Beth was elected captain, and she discovered that she had leadership skills. A year later she received a full college scholarship to dance on the University of Tennessee's dance team!

The irony of the scholarship was very unsettling to me. I had wanted Beth to be good in sports so that she could get an *athletic* scholarship. Instead, she was good in dance and ended up getting a scholarship anyway. If I had been raising Beth by myself, she never would have found dancing, felt competent at something, or received a scholarship!

Help your child explore to find something he or she feels competent in and enjoys. It just may be the best gift you ever give your child.

3. "Am I normal?"

Our children have a *need* to feel normal, or accepted, in their peer group. For us parents, this can be a double-edge sword. We want our children to feel normal—as long as the peer group has the same values as ours. We also want our children to be strong enough to say no when asked to do things that are "off point." Again, we must remember that we are our children's models. Our friendships with other adults serve as a model for our children. We must ask ourselves if it is a model we want our children to follow. We must make sure that our friends share our values and allow us to feel normal, too.

As I've mentioned previously, Curt was a happy and well-adjusted child when we lived in Pittsburgh. Then, when he was in fourth grade, we moved to Spartanburg, South Carolina. Being shy and uncomfortable around strangers made it difficult for him to make new friends. Finally, after two years of being rejected by his peers, a boy named Vance decided he wanted to be Curt's friend. Vance was not in the popular clique, but he was a native of Spartanburg and was well liked. As we got to know Vance, we also got to know his parents. They made Curt feel like a member of their own family. We all laughed together when we found out that Vance was one of the guys who had tormented Curt so much during our first year there. Fortunately, because Vance didn't play tennis, he and Curt never competed athletically.

After being friends for three years, it was difficult for the boys to say good-bye when it was time for our family to move once again. Vance came to our house and watched the movers put the last boxes into the van. Curt cried in the car as we headed to a new life in Nashville.

Although it was one year before Curt made another real friend in Nashville, he didn't have much time to feel sorry for himself because he was so active in school sports. Still, the feeling of acceptance that comes from friends was missing. Then, one day he met another excellent tennis player, Andy, who also was a freshman. Curt and Andy became doubles partners, and they never lost a match during their first year together. Just when Curt was beginning to feel accepted, summer came and Andy quietly drifted away. It seemed that Andy had a lot of friends, and Curt was only his tennis partner. Curt was hurt. Unfortunately, I made things worse—as parents sometimes do—by allowing Curt's hurt to become my hurt as well. I made it clear to everyone that Andy wasn't the nice guy everyone thought he was. Actually, I couldn't have been more wrong. I now know that Andy never intended to hurt Curt; he simply had never been "the new kid" and didn't know how much his friendship had meant to Curt.

Today, Andy works at a youth tennis camp every summer and sponsors inner city kids in Curt's name. We get letters from his students every year. I had clearly misjudged Andy, but I was blinded by the hurt that comes from watching your child hurt. Thankfully, during that difficult time, Carol and I did many of the right things. We made sure Curt could say yes to the other two questions. We made sure that he kept his friendship with Vance and with his cousin, Drew. Still, if I had had more confidence in my parenting skills, I could have helped Curt through his pain.

Then, one day, another young man decided to be Curt's friend.

His name was Lance, and he was one year younger than Curt. I had met Lance's parents at a tennis tournament. After much prodding, Carol and I convinced Curt to ask Lance to go water skiing. He accepted the invitation, and for the next three years, Curt had a best friend. They played on the tennis team together and even played doubles together in statewide tournaments. Lance had the incredible ability to not allow Curt's competitiveness to come between them. Once again, his friend's parents had a huge role to play in Curt's development. He fondly referred to them as Mr. and Mrs. Cleaver.

When Curt left for college a few years later, he felt accepted by his family, his community, *and* his friends. His athletic accomplishments had helped him to feel competent, his church and family friends had helped him to feel loved and loving, and several close friendships had helped him to feel "normal" in the eyes of his peers. This feeling of total acceptance allowed him to feel God's love in its purest sense. He no longer had to settle for the minister telling him that God loved him; he knew himself that it was true.

Although we can't ensure that our children will always feel normal in the eyes of their peers, we can help to comfort them and "fill the void" created when they are excluded by their peers. And when it comes to helping them feel loved, loving, and competent, we can have tremendous influence.

Remember That a Child Never Outgrows the Need for Nurturing

Generally speaking, our society does a fairly good job of nurturing young children. Yes, there are many exceptions, but overall, we nurture young children during the elementary school years. My own experience in public schools bears this out. Each year I visit over forty elementary schools, and I have yet to find one that does not do a wonderful job nurturing its students. I've observed that, without exception, the relationships between the adults and the children are very strong. The children trust their teachers and respect their leaders.

Unfortunately, I can't say the same of the middle schools and high schools I've visited, where I have sensed a big difference in relationships between students and faculty. In many cases, the trust is gone. It almost seems as if some faculties consider middle school to be boot camp and high school to be war.

Many adults are surprised by my observation, particularly those who do not have children in middle or high school. The fact is, children need nurturing throughout adolescence—and even into adulthood. Though the form of this nurturing should change as your children age, it still must be a high priority so that our children feel loved, accepted, supported, and cherished. Let's consider some of the ways you can nurture your maturing child.

1. Remember your own adolescence.

An important first step is to be more sensitive to our teenagers' need for nurturing. One of the best ways to do this is to remember our own travels down the rocky road of adolescence. Like me, you probably can recall a few "bumps" along the road, as well as times of smooth, easy traveling. And in those times of smooth traveling, you probably had a few nurturing adults in your life. As I recall my own journey, I realize that a major "bump" occurred my first year of high school; and I might not have recovered from that bump if I hadn't had several nurturing teachers during the remainder of my high school years.

My neighborhood high school, unlike most, began with the seventh grade. Because our community was small, we had only fifty students or so in each grade level. So, when I was in the seventh grade, the school decided to separate the students based upon IQ scores. I was put into the "smart" class with two other boys and twenty-two girls. Instantaneously, we three boys were hated by all of the other boys in seventh grade. We were bullied unmercifully. Unfortunately, our teacher never sensed the anger that had developed in us. There wasn't one adult in the school we felt comfortable talking to. The bullies would write nasty things about us on the blackboard in our homeroom, and our teacher would simply erase the words without making a comment. Meanwhile, our parents were bubbling with pride because we were in the smart class. This "hell on earth" continued through eighth grade as well. However, in ninth grade, we were sent to a new school, which was four times larger than our former school and full of new kids from other areas of the county. Although my self-esteem and self-worth were at an all-time low and I had become extremely shy, my life soon returned to normal. I was surprised by the friendliness of the other students. Although they had been together since kindergarten, they welcomed me into their groups. The teachers also sensed that I needed some encouragement, and I received plenty.

I'll never forget my Algebra II teacher, Miss McCrum. She was single, old, and proud of those two accomplishments. She also was the meanest looking woman I had ever seen. She carried her pack of cigarettes under the sleeve of her rolled up T-shirt. Her stern appearance was only heightened by the fact that she was the captain of the school's rifle team.

On the first day of class, Miss McCrum handed out wooden slide rules. She told us to guard them with our lives. Rumor had it that you would lose your life if you lost the slide rule. I guarded this wooden calculator with my life, keeping it in my briefcase at all times unless I was using it. One day after using it at home, I forgot to put it away and left it on my bed. Later that evening, my dog, Snoopy, wanted to play fetch. Instead of dropping a stick at my feet, he dropped my half-eaten slide rule. Ugh! I knew I was a dead soldier. As I expressed my anger at the dog, I heard these comforting words from my parents: "If you had put the slide rule away in its proper place, this would not have happened. This is your fault, not the dog's." Oh, how much better I felt! For the rest of the evening, I tried to generate an excuse that would help me stay alive. My parents kept telling me to tell the truth. Ugh!

I had already learned that if you were going to face death, you should do it first thing. So the next morning I went boldly into homeroom. "Miss McCrum," I said, "I need to talk to you." She never looked up. "I have something I need to tell you," I said. Again, she didn't look up. I pulled the slide rule out of my briefcase. As I pointed it toward her, I uttered what I knew would be my final words: "My dog, Snoopy, chewed my slide rule." She looked up, and when she saw the slide rule, she burst out laughing. I was amazed that her face didn't crack. "Aren't dogs the cutest things you have ever seen? My dog gets into trouble all the time. Here, give it to me, and I'll give you a new one in class today. Oh, by the way, Jimmy, if you ever need help, just come and see me."

Miss McCrum started class that day by announcing that Mr. Williams's slide rule had been ruined. My classmates looked at me with either sorrow or glee. She then pulled my slide rule out of her desk drawer; and as she held it up, she told the class with much joy that Snoopy had eaten my slide rule. Then she gave me a new one.

After that day, many of us in Miss Crum's Algebra II class began asking questions, and our grades improved. From that day on, we knew that Miss McCrum was a human being, not a great ogre! As I later learned, discipline, high expectations, accountability, and love are wonderful ways for adults to nurture children. And this nurtured student finished the course with an A.

I encourage you to reflect on your childhood and identify how nurtured you felt as you aged. Identify the kinds of people who were instrumental in your life. Identify the types of activities you enjoyed—and didn't enjoy. Then, you will be better equipped to see your children's world. When it comes to nurturing, today's world isn't much different from the world of our youth. All children need nurturing on a daily basis.

2. Spend more time communicating with your teen.

According to research concerning the behavior of children in early adolescence, most children start to pull away from their parents as they enter their teens. Most parents make the mistake of allowing this to happen. Instead, we need to maintain a close relationship with our teens. I am not suggesting that you keep them on a short leash and keep them from assuming greater responsibilities and more independence. What I am suggesting is that you not allow their independence to keep you from being an important part of their lives. Their growing independence should not keep you from having daily communication with your teens.

As you'll recall, Stephen Covey discovered that most parents spend only fifteen minutes a day communicating effectively with each child. If that isn't bad enough, he also discovered that when children become teens, this time actually decreases—with moms spending an average of nine minutes a day per child and dads spending an average of six minutes. Recently, a mom exclaimed, "I can't believe it! I have to spend more time with my children as they get older, not less!" I responded that the task is not insurmountable. In fact, if we follow the communication suggestions in chapter 8 (weekly family meetings and family quiet time, extended one-on-one times on weekends, and fun, family-based activities), we'll be on our way!

3. Ensure that your child has three or four positive adult role models.

As I've mentioned, it's important for our children to maintain ongoing relationships with caring adults throughout their growing up years. As children near the teen years, it becomes increasingly important for them to have adult role models in their lives other than Mom or Dad. The Search Institute, an organization that studies the behavior of children who stay on path, recommends that every young person needs three or four positive adult role models.

As I mentioned earlier in the chapter, I had several teachers in high school who were positive role models for me. I also had a wonderful tennis coach who was caring and kind and yet a disciplinarian when it came to practice. He always made us feel good about ourselves whether we won or lost. I had two wonderful youth directors. I had the parents of my two best friends who treated me as their son.

Likewise, Curt had an incredible tennis coach who was incredibly strict and demanding yet very caring and nurturing. Beth had several dance instructors who were very skillful in teaching dance as well as very nurturing and caring. She also had a wonderful academic advisor who helped her through the difficult time after she lost her fiancé. All of these adult role models enjoyed working with young people and took great pride in their students' achievements.

Extended family members can also serve as role models. In our family, grandparents and aunts and uncles all served as role models for Curt and Beth. Encourage your children to get to know these important adults and to seek their advice regularly. (Obviously, if the values of a particular relative or other adult contradict your own, then this individual is not a good choice for a role model.)

Remember That Adults Need Nurturing, Too

Many people have marveled at my ability to bounce back after setbacks—to get back on point. This is largely because I have been nurtured throughout my life, and I will need to be nurtured until the day I leave this earth. Unfortunately, I have met numerous adults who have not been nurtured, and, consequently, their "light" has gone out. This light is a reflection of the soul. They have lost sight of their North Star, and they have lost the warmth that comes from feeling God's love on a daily basis. Nurturing helps us to feel loved, and we never outgrow the need to feel loved. As adults, however, we must take a more proactive role in our own nurturing process in order to remove the many barriers we create that make us feel separated from God's love. You might say that we must actively pursue nurturing. Here are a few ways we can do just that.

1. Maintain your relationship with God.

Although I've discussed the subject throughout this book, I cannot overemphasize the importance of maintaining a relationship with God. Personal quiet time, prayer, and Bible study are important aspects of maintaining this relationship, as is church involvement. I mentioned earlier in the chapter that having a church home has filled the void in the life of my family and helped us to feel close to God. Likewise, I've mentioned previously that I feel it's important for *every* family not only to attend worship together, but also to participate in Sunday school and at least one other church activity. These activities, along with devotional time at home, help us to maintain a close relationship with God. As a result, our souls are nurtured and our stress levels are decreased. Some people choose to nurture themselves and relieve their stress on Sunday mornings in a different way, sleeping in or playing tennis or golf with a friend. I support the activities themselves, but not at the expense of one's church life and relationship with God. Nothing is more important.

2. Reduce the stress in your life associated with "providing" for your family.

I've said it before and I'll say it again: Much of our stress comes from our jobs. Specifically, the "anti-Christ" that has dimmed the light within many parents is the stress caused by materialism. The stress that comes from the pressure of meeting family needs and wants is truly a fire extinguisher. In the previous chapter, I mentioned Stephen Covey's recommendation that two-parent families have no more than 1.5 jobs. In other words, if both parents must work, one should have only a part-time job. Yet many families feel trapped because their fixed expenses are such a large percentage of their total income, leaving them little room for "downsizing"—or so they think. Take a look again at the Parent Point on page 158, "Finding a More Family-Friendly, Fulfilling Job." When many parents get to step 5, which is adjusting to a new and often lower level of income, they throw in the towel. A couple who attended one of my retreats was facing that very decision.

The father had lost his job and had not been able to find another one. The mother did not work outside the home, and the children attended private school. During my discussions with the father, I asked him what kind of job he would really like to do. He said that he wanted a job that allowed him to work with children. I told him that if he was really serious, I could help him find one. I explained, however, that the jobs I know about pay far less than corporate positions. As the couple discussed the subject, the mother said that because their fixed expenses were such a large percentage of their total income, she would have to find a job and they would have to take the children out of private school. The father's dream would have to wait for another day.

I could relate to their dilemma. During my four years in the Navy, I became very interested in drug education. Several young men in my unit were caught smoking marijuana, and I worked closely with the government during the investigation. Later, after leaving the Navy, I didn't have to find another job right away because Carol had a very good job working for the Navy as a computer programmer. I knew that if I wanted to go back to school to get my master's in counseling, I could. However, because my "darker" side said that I needed to find a well-paying job, I actively pursued employment. I went to a job fair held for military personnel, and after a successful interview with a large company, I was flown to Pittsburgh for additional interviews. When I was offered a good job, I jumped at it. I'll never know what my life would have been like if I had gone back to college and followed the "light" that was flickering inside. What I do know is that the stress and anger that came from my twenty-three years of service took a huge toll on my life and on my family. Like many of our friends, we kept buying more expensive homes as we moved from city to city; and as a result, our fixed expenses continued to increase, limiting our employment alternatives.

When was the last time you took a serious look at your monthly expenses? How many of these expenses are fixed? How many are variable? If you take all the expenses associated with your house or apartment and add them to your car and credit card payments, how much is left? If you have discovered that your fixed expenses are too consuming, then you need to make the hard decision and downsize your spending habits. Get rid of the large car note and buy an older used car. Reduce your mortgage by refinancing or buying a less expensive home. Eat more meals at home. I hope you get the idea. Once you have reduced your debt and your fixed expenses, you can afford to make the job changes that will allow you to enjoy your family more and, thus, enjoy life more. You'll find it's one of the best ways you can nurture yourself!

3. Maintain your own identity and take time for yourself.

How does a person find their true identity? It can be a very difficult task. When I took my corporate job, I was told I had a major fault that I needed to correct. I wore my feelings on my sleeve. So, for twelve years I worked on controlling my emotions and eventually became very successful at keeping my feelings inside. Unfortunately, when I went home, I also held my feelings inside. I will always remember a moment when Carol was expressing her concern about our marriage. She was crying and, at times, raising her voice in despair. I just sat there and analyzed her as if she were one of my customers. When I left the company and found a job that allowed me to be myself, I started once again to wear my feelings on my sleeve. The children and parents I work with seem to like this behavior very much. They always know where I stand with them.

Please don't allow your workplace to determine your identity. God created you and wants you to be *you*. Sure, you can work on some behavior issues, but your "core personality" comes from God and should not be changed just because your company *or anyone else* tells you to change.

I could write an entire book about taking time for yourself! Because I have addressed this subject in several chapters, I'll simply restate that we adults must take charge of ensuring that we have time for ourselves. It is very difficult to be nurtured when we never put ourselves in a position to receive that nurturing.

4. Maintain adult friendships.

One of the best ways to feel nurtured as adults is through adult relationships. I have learned, however, that most people have little time for adult friendships. Their lives are so hectic that they don't have enough time for their families or themselves. Thus, adult friends fall away.

Before Curt died, Carol and I had a wonderful group of friends. We all belonged to the same church and attended the same Sunday school class. After Curt's death, one of the couples really stepped up to the plate. Although they did not know Curt, they were able to offer us a lot of support, care, love, and kindness. In addition, I became a mentor for their two sons. My friendship with the boys helped me with Curt's absence. In time, he and his wife became active in the youth choir; and since Beth was in college at the time, we could not share that activity with them. So, before long, they found new friends and drifted away.

It's been over two years since we lost their friendship, and Carol and I have suddenly realized that we need a new couple or couples to replace our loss. We now realize how important it is for us to have nurturing adult companions. We have also learned how hard it is to find new adult friends. As I write this chapter, we are becoming proactive in our search. We are moving to a new neighborhood, a place where adults engage in adult activities. In addition, I am evaluating various organizations in which we might become active. We are also going to resume playing golf and tennis.

Isn't it amazing that even at the age of fifty-four, I am once again learning that you don't always value your friends until you lose them. If you find yourself in a similar situation, put a plan together that will help you find adult friends. Remember, we will need nurturing as long as we live.

5. Maintain relationships with young people.

I have found that maintaining relationships with young people—in addition to our own children—is another good way we adults can receive the nurturing we need. I first came to this realization when Curt's friends quit coming to our house after he died and I realized how much I had enjoyed being around them. Later, when I started working with young people on a daily basis, I realized that they were the kerosene that kept my light burning. When Beth went to college a few years later, I became close to some of her friends, particularly Heather, Leigh Ann, and Rachael. I fed off of their enthusiasm for life and their sense of caring for me. I only wish I had really known Beth's friends when she was younger. I could have had some wonderful opportunities to be a role model for them as well to be nurtured myself.

Parents often tell me they feel loved by their children's friends. Recently, a mother told me how lonely she has been since her son broke up with his girlfriend. The mom had enjoyed the companionship that came from this girl. She was fortunate to discover the joy that comes from developing a special relationship with a particular young person.

I began developing such a relationship several years ago when a special young man walked into my life—and I hope and pray he never leaves. His name is Will, and he was a fraternity brother of Curt's. He was only a freshman when Curt was killed. From time to time during his college career, he would give us a call. Because his grandparents and uncle live in Nashville, he often visited us when he came into town to see them. After graduation he got a job working for his uncle's law firm. I was very surprised because Will's major was child psychology. I told him that if he ever decided to leave the law office and pursue a job more in line with his major, all he needed to do was give me a call. By then I served on a council of agencies that worked with young people and worked closely with the United Way.

That day finally came. Will says that God finally helped him find his "true north." I wrote a letter of recommendation and sent Will's resume to several agencies. He had two job offers, and he chose to work for an agency that helps inner city children go to college. After one year, he became codirector of the agency.

Today I serve on the board of directors of Will's agency, and during the summer I work with his kids. As a result, we see each other all the time. He has become a second son for me as well as a second brother for Beth. Likewise, Beth is another sister for Will, and I am another friend and mentor.

There are many ways to create this kind of valuable relationship. In addition to Big Brothers and Big Sisters, there are wonderful boys and girls clubs as well as other youth-related organizations that constantly need adult mentors. There also are many young people in our local schools and even our neighborhoods who need a special adult in their lives. Look around: There may be one in your child's class or on your child's team. If you will take the time to nurture a relationship with this young person, you will discover that you will be nurtured in returned—oftentimes, two- or threefold!

Please, please, please nurture your children every day—even after they're teenagers and don't seem to need it. The truth is, that's when they need it more than ever. Keep their buckets full and apologize at the end of the day for any withdrawals you have made. Do what you can to help them feel competent, loved and loving, and accepted by their peers. Help them to find positive adult role models that share your values and learn the love language of your children. Spend more time talking to your children. Remind them often that you love them and that God loves them. And one more thing: Be sure to nurture yourself. It's difficult to nurture your children when you need nurturing yourself.

QUESTIONS TO PONDER

1. What are some things you do on a regular basis to put scoops of love into your children's buckets?

2. What are some things you do that empty your children's buckets?

3. Do you find it difficult to apologize to your children or ask them for forgiveness? If so, what can you do to improve in this important area?

4. How do you make love become a word of action in your family?

5. Can each of your children say yes to Laura Session Stepp's three key questions?

6. Do you know the love language of each of your children?

7. What can you do to reestablish or nurture relationships with other adults?

8. Do you have young people in your life who nurture you? If not, what can you do to change this?

BIBLIOGRAPHY

Books

Facts, Feelings, Family, and Friends: Alcohol and Other Drug-Use Prevention Through Life Skills Development, Linda Christensen. Edina, Minn.: Johnson Institute, 1990.

The Five Love Languages of Children, Gary Chapman and Ross Campbell. Chicago: Northfield Publishing, 1997.

How to Father, Dr. Fitzhugh Dodson. New York: Signet, 1974.

How to Talk So Kids Will Listen & Listen So Kids Will Talk, Adele Faber and Elaine Mazlish. New York: Avon Books, 1980.

Our Last Best Shot: Guiding Our Children Through Early Adolescence, Laura Sessions Stepp. New York: Riverhead Books, 2000.

Parenting Isn't for Cowards, Dr. James C. Dobson. Nashville: Word Publishing Group, 1987.

Parenting with Love and Logic: Teaching Children Responsibility, Foster Cline and Jim Fay. Colorado Springs: Pinon Press, 1990.

Parents, Teens, and Boundaries: How to Draw the Line, Jane Bluestein. Deerfield Beach, Fla.: Health Communications, Inc., 1993.

Peer Pressure Reversal: An Adult Guide to Developing a Responsible Child, Sharon Scott. Amherst, Mass.: Human Resource Development Press, Inc., 1985.

Raising Self-Reliant Children in a Self-Indulgent World, H. Stephen Glenn and Jane Nelsen. Roseville, Calif.: Prima Publishing Co., 1989.

Reviving Ophelia: Saving the Selves of Adolescent Girls, Mary Pipher. New York: Ballantine Books, 1994.

The 7 Habits of Highly Effective Families, Stephen Covey. New York: Franklin Covey Company, 1997.

The Shelter of Each Other: Rebuilding Our Families, Mary Pipher. New York: Ballantine Books, 1996.

The Strong-Willed Child, James Dobson. Wheaton, Ill.: Tyndale, 1978.

What Kids Need to Succeed: Proven, Practical Ways to Raise Good Kids, Peter L. Benson, Judy Galbraith, and Pamela Espeland. Minneapolis, Minn.: Free Spirit, 1997.

Winning the Parenting Game: Putting Family First, Deloris Jordan. New York: Harper & Row, 1996.

The Wounded Spirit, Frank Peretti. Greenville, Miss.: Word Publishing, 2000.

"You Can't Make Me" (But I Can be Persuaded), Cynthia Ulrich Tobias. Colorado Springs: Waterbrook Press, 1999.

Videos

The Broken Toy. Summerhills Production. Copyright 1993 by Thomas Brown (800-477-8277).

Parent to Parent: Parenting for Safe and Drug-Free Youth, Bill Oliver. The Passage Group.

Parenting for Prevention: How to Help Kids Be Sensible, Safe, and Secure. © 1998 - Hazeldon Foundation, Center City, MN.

Raising Children Who Turn Out Right, Tim Kimmel. © 1997 by Sampson Ministry Resources, Dallas.

Set Straight on Bullies. Copyright 1988 by National School Safety Center. (805-373-9977) www.nssc1.org.